UPROAR

UPROAR

CALM LEADERSHIP IN ANXIOUS TIMES

Peter L. Steinke

ROWMAN & LITTLEFIELD
Lanham • Boulder • New York • London

Published by Rowman & Littlefield
An imprint of The Rowman & Littlefield Publishing Group, Inc.
4501 Forbes Boulevard, Suite 200, Lanham, Maryland 20706
www.rowman.com

6 Tinworth Street, London SE11 5AL, United Kingdom

Distributed by NATIONAL BOOK NETWORK

British Library Cataloguing in Publication Information Available

Library of Congress Cataloging-in-Publication Data

Names: Steinke, Peter L., author.
Title: Uproar : calm leadership in anxious times / Peter L. Steinke.
Description: Lanham : Rowman & Littlefield, [2019] | Includes bibliographical
   references and index.
Identifiers: LCCN 2018039885 (print) | LCCN 2018051490 (ebook) | ISBN
   9781538116548 (ebook) | ISBN 9781538116531 (pbk. : alk. paper)
Subjects: LCSH: Leadership—Psychological aspects.
Classification: LCC BF637.L4 (ebook) | LCC BF637.L4 S8256 2019 (print) |
   DDC 158/.4—dc23
LC record available at https://lccn.loc.gov/2018039885

♾️™ The paper used in this publication meets the minimum requirements of American National Standard for Information Sciences—Permanence of Paper for Printed Library Materials, ANSI/NISO Z39.48-1992.

Printed in the United States of America

CONTENTS

INTRODUCTION

For more than twenty-five years, I have worked with small and large systems from a variety of professional viewpoints: first as the minister of several churches, next as the director of a program for emotionally troubled youth, the director of two counseling centers supported by a social service agency and a hospital, an adjunct professor, and finally a consultant to organizations.

I was fortunate to discover the Post Graduate Seminar in Family Emotional Process in Bethesda, Maryland, under the tutelage of Dr. Edwin Friedman, author of *A Failure of Nerve: Leadership in the Age of the Quick Fix*. He introduced me to the Bowen family system theory. The system perspective gave me the vantage point from which to view emotional process, whether I was observing a family, a congregation, a hospital, an educational unit, a small business, or a large company. I learned that six major triggers incited anxiety in these systems, and no one trigger affected the emotional system more than the leadership, whether the leaders were parents, priests, principals, presidents, board chairpersons, owners, or chief operating officers. How any one of them handled self in the emotional system was more determinate than anything else in terms of outcome. Critical to all situations was the degree of responsibility expressed in the system.

You will observe how leaders impact a system by

- separating themselves from the surrounding anxiety
- making decisions based on principle, not instinct
- taking responsibility for their own emotional being
- regulating their own anxiety in the face of sabotage or resistance
- staying connected to others, even those who disagree with them
- choosing self-directed goals
- being a non-anxious presence
- supplying an immune response to pathogenic forces (invasiveness)
- focusing on emotional processes rather than the symptoms they produce
- not allowing the most dependent to be in control
- knowing that people naturally influence one another
- recognizing leader and follower as complements, parts of the whole
- realizing that insight, love, and reasonableness are not adequate for change in an anxious system
- accepting that mature leadership does not always work, that immaturity is too embedded in the system

The overall health and functioning of any organization depends primarily on one or several people at the top who can exercise the above characteristics well.

Despite the rash of books written on leadership in the last two or three decades, we have not seen an increment in effective leadership throughout the institutional world. Religious leaders were slow to acknowledge sexual predation among priests; political leaders continued to serve their donors' needs and their own reelection. Business figures were indicted for deceptive practices. Colleges and universities protected faculty and students who preyed on others. Researchers fudged their results or hid them from public view. Locally, citizens heard reports of malfeasance by those in positions of authority. Long repressed (for diverse reasons), many individuals exposed those in leadership positions who had sexually harassed or abused them.

It is known that the key characteristic of a pathogenic force is invasiveness: violating the space, dignity, and emotional well-being of others. Viruses, demagogues, parasites, bullies, sexual predators, and name-calling blamers function in the same way. They have no boundaries, they do not respect the boundaries of others (and obviously go where they don't belong), they must have it their own way, and they never learn from their experience. Being in a role of leader, one may be tempted more than others to be a transgressor or trespasser if one thinks of self as entitled or special.

Perhaps more important, the leadership literature has addressed leadership from a faulty base: leaders have certain personality traits, exercise an authoritarian presence, enjoy the competitive world, possess more knowledge and data, have fingertip answers, demonstrate boldness, and are strangers to self-doubt. Absent from the discussion of leadership is the capacity to work through emotional processes. If emotion is mentioned, it's a retardant to thinking, or if placed in a positive light, emotion becomes part of a technique to motivate people to do something. One will scarcely read about the interplay between emotion and cognition in decision making. Processing information (how we hear, what questions we ask, etc.), we think, travels one way on Thought Street. Yet, what we do, think, and feel is tinged with the emotional, "the hidden agenda."

No doubt, we can attribute some of this to the fact that most books on leadership are written by men who would rather live as if they are in control, not prone to flashes of instinct or purveyors of mindless action.

From a fresh perspective, Murray Bowen asserts that the emotional system is elemental to the whole human enterprise, and he addresses what leaders can do to impact the system with clarity, conviction, differentiation, presence, and calm functioning. Further, his student Dr. Edwin Friedman noted how leaders today suffer a "failure of nerve" by giving quick fixes, which simply gives leveraging power to the most immature, dependent, and recalcitrant individuals. By pleasing their lizard brain, the leader, unaware, is operating from the same lesser neurological base. Friedman notes that the quick fix eliminates the opportunity to challenge people to grow and be responsible and responsive people. Instant solutions favor the neediness of people. Even more, when leaders manipulate, lie, or play on people's anger and frustration for self-gain, the lizard brain has its glorious moment.

Our word for leader is derived from the Old English word *laeden*, which has antecedents with the Dutch *leiden* and the German *leiten*. It means to go, depart, travel, and guide. Leadership that caters to emotional needs (reduction of pain, fast relief, certainty) is in league with survival, not challenge. Leading implies movement. There has to be a shift in the emotional processes of the system, or imaginative gridlock ensues. Being curious, imagining, and reframing is as much emotional as cognitive.

Our systems have too many leaders who are echoes, ditto marks, pleasers, Manichean, and unimaginative. Our systems need to produce leaders that take the first step, persevere through predictable demands for comfort, and do not crater to resistance and sabotage, who can separate themselves from the anxious climate, who can have the nerve to exchange certainty and survival for imagination and adventure. None of this is possible with the old paradigm of data, technique, and expertise; it will mean plowing into the emotional processes that are part of the human endeavor, buttressed by calm reflectiveness, and not letting automatic resistance hold you back. We have had for our use tons of data that other generations hardly approximated, and yet the tonnage has not advanced our level of maturity. We still get locked down in old survival needs.

In a time of Uproar, we need leaders who can approximate mature actions. But training programs in leadership still concentrate on know-how, skill sets, and data. Expertise, technique, and a focus on others seem to be immovable parts of the training syllabus for leaders. Instead, Bowen would have you focus on your presence, self-awareness, and being a responsible and responsive self. How you handle yourself in times of change, ambiguity, or adversity is the touchstone of leadership. It is not how you persuade, cajole, or mandate others to behave.

For a leader, crisis will arise. All the factors that contribute to functioning in a self-differentiated (mature) manner will resolve the crisis in fundamental ways not attainable by quick fixes or elastic promises. Any social system—a family, workplace, or even a whole society—improves when people function less and less in reactive ways and more and more on the basis of values and beliefs sustained by clear goals. Differentiation is a lifelong process, a capacity to be in relationship to others without being ruled by one's own or others' emotional reactivity. Dr. Friedman noted that "the key to the kingdom" is understanding that differences do not cause differing. The messiness comes with the emotionality that is attached to contentious issues or upsetting context. Actively relating to those on opposite sides and remaining free of the emotional field is the gift a leader brings to the system.

Bowen did not recommend straddling the fence or functioning like a wet noodle. Actively relating to others without emotional baggage allows one to be freer, more flexible, broader in perspective, more capable of inserting calm reflection and engaging others on a thinking level. Uproar requires mature leaders who will deal with lots of immaturity, reactivity, and other survival behaviors. I learned Bowen theory from Rabbi Edwin Friedman over a period of nine years. I have distinguished how Friedman understood the theory and how Bowen presented it. Also, I inserted my own experiences and perception of the theory. You may find some explanations or verbiage advanced by Friedman or myself. One reviewer of the manuscript voiced what others mentioned: "You put legs on the theory."

This book is arranged into four sections with three chapters in each. At the end of the chapters, I have placed the Leader's Notebook, a short section to illustrate, enrich, or engage your thinking about family systems thinking and leadership.

The names of individuals, businesses, and other identity markers have been changed to protect those who were originally involved. Situations have been slightly altered in a few cases for the same reason.

I want to acknowledge those who have graciously assisted in the formation of the book: my wife Kelly, who is a visual artist and offered one of her larger paintings for the book cover design; the late Ray Johnson for use of several visuals; likewise, my son Tim who created a couple of cartoons; and the following people who offered insights and suggestions—Eddie Sharp, John Hirsch, Kathy Wiseman, Dana Stokes, Dan Biles, Gloria Beth Amodeo, Tod Bolsinger, and Roger Schwarze. A special expression of gratitude is due to Serena Verzhinsky who typed the manuscript and, in spite of my changes, stayed calm no matter what.

I

THE NEW CONTEXT

*Now there are times when a whole generation is caught . . .
between two ages, two modes of life, with the consequence that
it loses all power to understand itself and has no standards,
no security, no simple acquiescence.*

—Herman Hesse

*You wake up one day and say: "Everything is slipping
away." My culture. You can't say "Christmas" anymore;
you have to say "Happy Holidays." There's been some mu-
tation, and you just don't feel like you're on the same page
with what's been going on the past thirty years.*

—Girard Amen

*Every few hundred years in Western history, there occurs
a sharp transformation. Within a few short decades, society—its worldview, its basic values, its social and political
structures, its art, its key institutions—rearranges itself.
We are currently living through such a time.*

—Peter Drucker

1

LIVING NOWHERE
BETWEEN TWO
SOMEWHERES

THE ROARING

Charles Dickens's famous opening statement in *A Tale of Two Cities* could be true of many periods in history:

> It was the best of times, it was the worst of times. It was the age of wisdom, it was the age of foolishness. It was the season of light, it was the season of darkness. It was the spring of hope, it was the winter of despair.[1]

And now, it is the best of times and the worst of times, but also the most tumultuous of times. Living nowhere between two somewheres has been called "the liminal experience," the "neutral zone," and the "transition space." My own term is "Uproar." It has more association with the emotional side of life. "America," journalist Brooke Gladstone said, "is so noisy these days." Many people want to have a voice in the vast confusion surfacing in American society. Uproar is a time of dislocation; everything is "up in the air" or "at loose ends." Societies regress in an atmosphere of anything goes. In America, we are sorting out our values and future course as we face immense disruptions, gnawing uncertainties, and new anxieties.

Under the siege of Uproar, our thinking capacities decline. We even use reason to justify the irrational. Our trusty inventory of opinions is imperiled. Truth is put on a seesaw; suspicion is overseeded. Polarized, groups find it difficult to converse without wielding emotional hatchets. Explosive tantrums throw respect to the wind. Ethics are stored in the attic—"out of sight, out of mind." God is reduced to a candy machine, easily nickled-and-dimed. Buffeted by lies, stable folks lose confidence in reality. Normal has become a backseat driver.

Take the commonsense matter of guns and mass shootings. Assault rifles are designed for aggression and violence, not self-defense. Regulation is needed, lest they get in the hands of the emotionally erratic. If you use this logic, though, others counter it with the fear that the real intent is to take away all guns. Who is against driving and regulating drivers? No one. Putting on a seatbelt is a law intended to protect people; it is not intended to strip away your driver's license.

Uproar unsettles conventional ways of relating. With the new technology, we connect mostly with our inner circle and expand contact with others in the outer ring, those with whom we share interests or from whom we purchase things. But the commonplace interactions, Marc Dunkelman notes (*The Vanishing Neighbor*), are disappearing—the contacts with familiar people, the exchanges with the grocer, the doctor, and the electrician. Sherry Turkle, once called the Margaret Mead of digital culture, points out that along with the advantages of the new technology come new anxieties (cf. *Alone Together*).

And Uproar affects our sense of coherence and stability. Blaming becomes endemic, and we wonder who is right. With tribalistic fervor, we retreat to partisan positions to secure a stationary base. We lose the meaning and direction of our lives. Researchers have discovered that when we do not have a compass, a map, a destination, or even a star to guide us, we walk in circles. An endless circling leads to the same space, as much a form of regression as walking backward.

No cohort of people have had to live with such velocity and reach of change as those who are currently living. If you would check a thesaurus, you would find these companion words for tumult: *messy, vulgar, strident, confusion, disorderly, noisy,* and *turbulent.* We are living at a time not like any other. Every generation, from Israel to Greece, from Rome to Victorian England, believes itself to be the fulfillment of Dickens's observation. But we Americans are an anxious lot, with nearly forty million suffering an anxiety disorder. In the World Mental Health Survey, Americans were the most anxious people in the fourteen countries studied, even more than people in Nigeria, Lebanon, and Ukraine. According to Google Trends, the number of web searches for the term *anxiety* has doubled in the last five years. College students are said to be more apprehensive than ever before. In her book, *iGEN*, Professor Jean Twenge surprisingly discovered that the iGeners "seem terrified."[2] Perhaps it is not facetious to say, as one commentator has, that we can make a strong case for being gold medalists in the Anxiety Olympics.

The naturalist E. O. Wilson defines Uproar succinctly:

> We have created a Star Wars civilization, with Stone Age emotions, medieval institutions, and godlike technology. We thrash about.[3]

Simpler yet, a British anthropologist calls our day "liquid." Solids and solidarities have disappeared. Other pundits have their favorite way of saying it: "the unraveling of society" (Charles Murray), "the bacchanal of disruption" (Ron Wieseltier), "paddling in the swamp" (Sharon Paloz Parks), "Everything everywhere" (William Knoke), and the poet's lament, "The blizzard of the world has overturned the order of the soul" (Leonard Cohen). We are "a generation that's going to be asked to dance in a hurricane" (*Kirkus Reviews*).

VULNERABILITY

Digital life, recession, two wars, worries about jobs, health care, our children's safety, nature's cataclysms, a tense presidential election and the aftermath of anxiety about who was elected, extremist groups, inequality of wealth, low trust in the people in charge, the nuclear threat, climate change, toxic water supplies, Zika, Ebola, or whatever new strain of germ appears, and sheer massive change—it's no wonder we spend over two billion dollars annually on antianxiety medications, not to mention the cost of other forms of anxiety reduction.

With uncertainty following us like our shadow, traditional social principles lose their capacity to capture people's attention and to inform their lives. People view relationships differently and experiment with alternate patterns of connecting. Living on the cliff of uncertainty, people succumb to conspiracy theories or accept the bizarre as reality, anything to dispel the terror of the unknown. "Uncertainty," neuroscientist Joseph LeDoux states, "is the breeding ground of anxiety." Encased in dread, our thinking capacities are blunted, and we believe the craziest things.

Misgivings about traditional leadership roles appear in Uproar. Being perceived as tied to the past, traditional leaders are poor guides for the swiftly shifting context. Many therefore gravitate to leaders who supply super simple solutions that extract complexity. People look for the literal, the either/or, and the straightforward, thereby eliminating loopholes, gaps, and uncertain trumpets.

We are prone to seek rescuers with puffed-up promises and rich remedies. We like the messianic figures, the odd and flamboyant, the iconoclasts, the smooth soothsayers, or any numinous evangelist. The times are ripe for a return to the old myth about the "hero-warrior" leader, one who will redeem or relieve the chaotic conditions and cool down our overheated anxiousness. "The harder life is," psychologist Keith Payne says, "the more miraculous it becomes." There has to be a magic kingdom with a wizard!

Although popular business writer Jim Collins warned that "looking for a savior" is the fourth of five stages in how systems fail, people nonetheless rely on their "survival instincts and fear," which "evoke lurching, reactive behavior." We indeed thrash about! In contrast, Collins suggests, "Breathe. Calm yourself. Think. Focus. Aim."[4]

EMOTIONAL PROCESS

Briefly, I introduce two of his concepts that need to be understood before expounding on them in later chapters. First, Bowen uses the word *emotional* to encompass all behavior that is governed by instinct. In emotional processes, we relate to one another impulsively. These automatic, biologically programmed, and innate forces control eating, reproducing, and self-preserving. Basically, these are lower-brain (sometimes called the lizard brain) functions. We share these neural structures with all animate life. The lower brain is hungry, horny, and scared. "When it comes to detecting and responding to danger, the brain . . . just hasn't changed much," LeDoux explains. "In some ways, we are emotional lizards."[5]

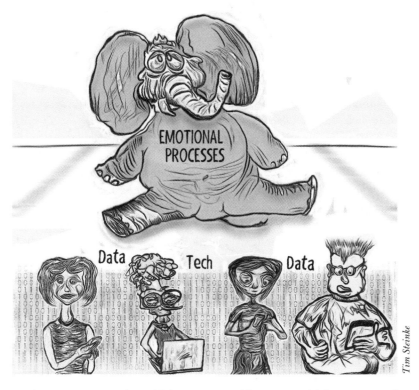

Humans are more than chickens, cats, and horses; we think, reason, and feel before we act. Animals do not read manuals on how to behave, nor do they think about things before they act. Instinct takes care of it all. But we make decisions that are scrutinized and make sense. Even then, we are subject to our impulses.

George Akerlof and Robert Shiller describe how "animal spirits" (a spontaneous urge to act) influence our decisions even in financial matters.[6] Anxiety can overpower thoughtfulness. We make spur-of-the-moment or anxious choices that are not necessarily economically wise or beneficial.

We like to regard ourselves as rational beings. Occasionally we are. No less, the Nobel Prize winner in economic science Richard Thaler has, like Akerlof and Shiller, pointed out that we substitute emotion for thought when making decisions about money and value. We won't pay more for an umbrella when it is raining. We place a higher value on something after we own it (the endowment effect). In addition, researcher Daniel Kahneman has studied our use of more than twenty heuristic devices to save energy (*heuristic* indicates a mental shortcut). For instance, we employ the "halo effect," an intuitive mechanism that attributes special abilities and unique strengths to celebrities and the wealthy, though in reality there is no proof for the attribution. We assume or intuit that their status had to come about because of their wisdom, success, or achievements.[7]

Systems, composed of people interacting and influencing one another, always exhibit emotional processes. When anxiety intensifies, multiplies, and paralyzes, we are dumber. We cannot see options, the big picture, or objective reality. We forfeit that which most defines our humanity. Since transitional times are incredibly random, uncertain, and disorienting, anxiety finds fertile ground. Then, feeling insecure, vulnerable, or at risk, nature provides the automatic reactions of fight, flight, or freeze, all in the service of survival. But if we cannot get beyond the emotional processes, calm reflection is not available to us. Uncertain, we tend to replace thought with emotion.

DIFFERENTIATION

As for leadership, until and unless you recognize the power of your own instinctual life, you will continue to assess outside conditions, persons, or ideas to be the cause of your or others' nervous unrest. So, in response, you use your energy to rectify, control, or eliminate the outside stimuli. You do this even though the real factor is anxiety. Dr. Edwin Friedman formed the equation HE = RO. HE stands for the hostility of the environment—the number and strength of stressors. RO represents the response of the organism. Will the leader focus on the external and threatening stressors or on what is happening within the self? Will the stressors be the determinant, or the one who engages them? Will one act first and think later, or think and then take action?

If the leader becomes anxious and forfeits calm reflection, the system is essentially leaderless. Anxiety tumbles down like loose rock dislodged from a high position. In a time of Uproar, the leader cannot be as anxious as everyone else.

Tim Steinke

To counteract automatic antics, you need to rise up out of the emotional muck. Bowen envisioned a lifelong process called "differentiation of self." The ability to be a separate self in a relationship system would allow you to be more reflective, less apprehensive, and more goal oriented. You will discover the meaning of differentiation in terms of definition, connection, regulation, and direction in a forthcoming chapter. What you need to know now is that Bowen borrowed the term *differentiation* from embryology. When a cell matures—when it becomes something specific, like a muscle, liver, or heart cell—it is said to be differentiated. A stem cell is an immature cell, not having developed into a definite kind or form. Differentiation is about maturity. Your maturity is determined by how well you balance two emotional needs of being separate and close. The temptation or danger is to lean toward one of the forces intensely and automatically, which leads to emotional cutoff or fusion. In the process, you lose balance and become less resilient in your responses. Instinct cramps your functioning.

Actually, the two needs are not oppositional but rather serve as a range of possibilities. You could become too distant or too close. There are perils on either side, too isolated or too entangled. Relationships require a balancing act, which is only possible when you know your own boundaries and respect those of others.

What does this mean for leadership functioning? Either the leader becomes unengaged with others (acts rigidly, dominates, withdraws, becomes overly dogmatic) or too close (panders, seeks consensus, shifts with the wind for the sake of harmony). Rather than leading from one's convictions and vision, the leader allows nonthinking and reflexive action to determine behavior.

In highly anxious times, people tend to tilt toward one or the other extreme in order to survive. They automatically withdraw or overly accommodate, whatever will preserve the organism or organization. Bowen offered an ideal way of functioning within these parameters:

- An effective leader has the courage to act on convictions in the midst of crisis or challenge.
- A leader will be interested in promoting the welfare of all alongside of his or her own well-being.
- Being a leader, one will be neither angry nor dogmatic.
- A leader refrains from telling others what they should do and focuses on regulating self.
- A leader respects the opinions of others but knows the difference between responsible and irresponsible thinking and acting.
- A leader functions with well-established beliefs or principles.
- A leader utilizes the strengths of others and is not depleted or resentful.

He summarizes the ideal in the phrase "the non-anxious presence." While anxiety is always a part of human functioning, Bowen is not suggesting that a leader be an emotional superman or superwoman. He is proposing that the leader be mature, which is only possible when one can be more calm in reflection and less reactive to people and events.

THE LEADER'S NOTEBOOK

Anxiety and Life Events

I have used the following chart to help leaders in a system look for symptoms generated by emotional forces. Under "Date," one could put months or years, depending on which is appropriate. Since disruptions are a key source of anxiety, columns are given to deletions, additions, and stressors. The last column is for noting celebrations, which are usually absent or sparse during anxious times.

In filling in the columns, you may note local, regional, national, or global events.

Date	Deletions	Additions	Stressors	Celebrations

2

ANXIOUS TIMES

The culture is rapidly waning as a widespread anxiety rises.

—Joseph Chilton Pierce

ANXIETY ON THE RISE

As a leader, you come to your position with enthusiasm and hope. Your commitment is genuine; you anticipate making a difference, much of which will be satisfying and enjoyable. You will be involved with routine oversight, ratifying changes, clarifying policies, settling disputes, and offering new challenges.

With a gradual or sudden elevation of anxiety in your system, a different tone or mood develops. You sense a shift of spirit; you hear rumblings. The usual lighthearted banter and general chatter gives way to serious silence. You are informed of some startling news or devious behavior. Your leadership role will take on a different dimension now. You are dealing with emotional forces.

Nothing complex or controversial happens without confusion, resistance, or emotional reactivity. All tensions, traumas, and transitions leave a trail of anxiety. This is where you enter the story. Anxiety alone will not harm or endanger a system. How anxiety is addressed will determine the outcome more than anything else. Your responsible and enlightened behavior is the touchstone.

ANXIETY AND REALITY

Stoic Bert Endren kept a lock on his emotions. Seldom would his face or voice reveal the sensations pulsing within. If affected, he would look into space motionless and remain mute.

"Are you OK, Bert? I had to do it."

His employer solemnly told Bert about his termination at Oceana Shipping Enterprise. Bert slowly stood up and walked to the office door.

"Bert, believe me, this was hard. Things change. We've been hit hard."

Not looking back, Bert left the office. "Bert," Wallace pleaded with him one last time.

Outside, Bert walked straight to his truck, opened the door, and put his head on the steering wheel, clutching it tightly. Twenty-two years, he thought to himself, and in a flash it was gone. He knew that sales had declined precipitously with people purchasing items online. Still, he thought his loyalty merited something—"Not me, not Bert." His daughter Allison had two more years of college to complete; his wife's cancer would become worse now, for sure.

A strange feeling came over him. His breathing shortened as his chest tightened. Coldness rippled through him, and he shivered. "I'll kill him," he thought recklessly. "I'll expose his secrets and kick his ass real good." With his stoicism cracking under strain, his emotions began to surface. He leaned back as if to awaken from sleep. He thought of destroying himself. For three hours, he ran solutions through his mind, none rational and all superficial.

Greta was startled when Bert came home in the early afternoon. Going into the garage, he mumbled something incoherently to her. Standing at his workbench, Bert moved items aimlessly. He drove his truck to the gas station, filling his tank with three and a half gallons and washing all the exterior glass. He came home and later that night told Greta he had been fired. She put her hands over her mouth: "No." They silently looked at each other. Then Bert looked down and said, "Who is going to hire someone fifty-three years old? Allison's school. Your health. Sucks the life out of you." The usual taciturn, self-confident Bert could no longer keep his emotions harnessed. He banged his fists on the table, and a couple of pieces of dinnerware fell to the floor. Greta covered her whole face with one hand and reached out for his with the other hand.

ANXIETY: AN ANATOMY

In Bert's case, the nervous strain was in no way pathological, though he had a penchant for shutting down emotionally. It was humanity in full emotional dress. Lacking anticipatory capacities, animals, we think, do not have anxiety; fear, yes, but that is a matter we will discuss later. The only human beings that are free of anxiety we call sociopaths. Obviously, anxiety is not a useless occurrence. At worst, it distorts our thinking.

Today we work through our personal anxiety and that which surrounds us—the fomenting of hate groups, the cleavage between red and blue states, the legislative impasse at the federal level, the immigration crisis, the national health care fiasco, and a multitude of other circumstances. Personally, we worry about relationships, finances, finding meaning in life, and health issues. Tomorrow's impending dilemmas are coming faster than ever before. If 47 percent, for instance, of the workforce is vulnerable to new uses for robotics, Bert's anxiety will become that of many. Then, too, it is estimated that 55 percent of current workers are financially unprepared for retirement. When someone suggested eliminating $800 billion from Medicaid, no one realized that three hundred hospitals would have to cease operation. For the marginal in society, best estimates say there is a 50 percent chance they can overcome their desolate situation. The fading influence of religious teaching on private and social behavior, while slowly being replaced by secular humanism, could create a moral vacuum, absent a moral foundation.

A recent neuroscience study uncovered how threatening information invades and takes over working memory (short-term memory). Anxious people tend to perceive their world in a more threatening way, even in the absence of immediate threat. They spend excessive time thinking about potential danger in safe situations. The high nervous group allocate working memory resources to threat and, in the meantime, overtax it, interfering with sleep, listening, and reflective thought. Anxiety likes to have a lot of elbow room.

Earlier, psychologists held to the idea that anxiety stemmed from the newborn's separation from the safe womb of mother, and all further separations reenacted the original loss. A pair of researchers, the Lynds, in their well-known study called "Middletown," attributed the rise of anxiety to the massive changes happening all at once in all sectors of life.

Political commentators saw the rise of fascism coming from widespread anxiety in society. Having a desperate need for relief, people turned to authoritarian figures, entranced by their dashing promises and steel-like confidence. They would reverse misfortune into fortune, a vacuous life into a full one.

In 1950, the poet W. H. Auden wrote the poem "The Age of Anxiety." He associated loneliness with anxiety:

> Alive but alone, belonging—where?—
> Unattached like a tumbleweed.[1]

The sociologist Philip Slater put it to prose in *The Pursuit of Loneliness*, citing the loss of bonds between people in the new postindustrial world. Theologian Paul Tillich attributed anxiety to three human experiences: the awareness of death, the sense that life is meaningless, and "fate" or the uncertainty of life.

Psychologist Rollo May tied it all together in *The Meaning of Anxiety*. He acknowledged that anxiety is "essential to the human condition." Anxiety excites the instinctual reactions of fight, flight, and freeze. It races the heart and runs rapidly through the nervous system. Anxiety has survival value. At low levels it can keep you from being careless, motivate change, warn you about possible danger, and rev up your body for action. With intensity, frequency, and duration, however, anxiety stifles rather than prompts.

Taking a look at *anxiety*'s family tree, you get a sense of its power to affect your life. The great-grandfather is *ango*, which means "to press together." Our English word for anxiety derives from the Latin *angere* (to cause pain by squeezing). In almost every language, the word for anxiety comes from a word signifying wind or air, choking or strangling, or the physical area of the neck. A common symptom for those who suffer anxiety disorders is the difficulty of breathing.

Anxiety's cousins include the following:

angustus (anguish), Latin
eng (narrow), German
angr (anger), Old Norse
angst (dread), German
angina (upper chest pain), Latin
argh (to strangle), Indo-European
ananke (chain, yoke), Greek

Ananke was the name for the Greek god of constraining who presided over slavery (slaves bore chains around their necks called *ananke*). In eastern parts of the world (Cambodia and Vietnam), anxiety is associated with the wind. In Hebrew, *zarar* is translated "distress," but it literally means "a narrow space." But *yasha*, its opposite ("open space"), is the source for the words "salvation" and "yeshua."

It is a family of words that expresses narrowness, tightness, and suffocation. Anxiety can take us by the throat, choke the life out of us, and chain us like slaves. Of course, when unencumbered, we say life is "a breeze," or we had a "blast," indicating a sense of freedom, ease, and drive.

TRIGGERS AND CONSEQUENCES

Before, I mentioned that fear and anxiety are different experiences, though we often use them interchangeably. Fear is connected to a specific threat, like spiders or snakes, closed or open spaces. There is an object involved. Anxiety, on the other hand, is more generalized, subjective, and anticipated. Anxiety: "Start worrying. Details to follow." There is no devil or villain activating it. What goes through your mind is that anything can happen at any time. What you cherish is disposable. Anxiety is objectless, lacking an identifiable force or feature. It is an uneasiness beyond any clear cause; it is an indefinite, vague apprehension. Author Jodi Picoult compared anxiety to a rocking chair, saying that it gets you going, but you don't get anywhere.

Anxiety affects your functioning in many negative ways:

- creates "imaginative gridlock," limiting what is seen, heard, or understood;
- forecloses the realm of options, alternatives, and possibilities;
- decreases your capacity to learn;
- increases your demand for certainty and arouses feelings of inadequacy;
- focuses your attention away from self to external factors;
- magnifies differences;
- migrates and perpetuates itself like an infection;
- leads to an array of defensive behaviors;
- unleashes blaming of others;
- prepares you to sell your soul to some miraculous cure or larger-than-life figure; and
- postpones patience and leads to foolish decisions.

The severity of the outcomes depends on whether or not your anxiety is acute or chronic. Acute anxiety, being time-bound and situational, has a lesser effect on your functioning. Momentarily you lose your poise, but you regain it quickly. Chronic anxiety is always set to go off. No matter what issue is being contested, what interpretation is being discussed, or what idea divides people, the anxiety alarm is ready to sound. Essentially, the chronicity relates to a person's inability to regulate one's own emotional capacities. Instinct has a headlock on intent.

The triggers of anxiety are manifold: money, trauma, betrayal, difficult people, and unemployment, to name a few. But I have discerned six common triggers that affect everyone and every system. Sometimes these triggers come in pairs or more.

- Disruptions (change, loss, separation, innovation, accidents)
- Feeling trapped (helpless, hopeless, powerless, not able to influence an outcome)
- Threat (real or imagined, sensing potential harm or injury, survival instincts take over, "a wolf at the door")
- Differences (opposites, strangeness, diversity, contrasting ideology, values, race/ethnicity)

- Uncertainty (doubts, ambiguity, the unknown, the unpredictable)
- Depletion (lessening, deficiency, exhausting, wearing down)

It is helpful if leaders are aware of the major triggers that affect them individually or the system in general. The emotional side of life operates on its own and has plenty of leeway to react to things. But if one can be aware of the trigger most likely to create reaction, regulation is possible to a greater degree. No awareness, no choice. With conscious control, you can veto, modify, or stifle the impulsive push. Still, we are neurologically designed with survival instincts, having more neurons extending from the lower brain to the upper than the other way around. Intuition has an advantage over intention.

NOT AS FAST

When people live through a time of Uproar, the conversation about leadership gains greater importance. Our anxiety plays a role in how we think, feel, and act. Knowing that anxiety, like leaking water, flows down, leaders cannot be as anxious as everyone else. Because of the infectious nature of anxiety, the leader's apprehensiveness contaminates the whole system.

The contamination can take several forms. Normally, we think that contested arguments or disturbing events are primary and the emotional factors secondary. In Bowen theory, though, the emotionality is primary. Differences by themselves do not cause differing. The amount and persistence of the emotional forces create the dissension and division. Unless and until these forces are dealt with, the differing continues. So many leaders will focus attention on how to change or settle the issues instead of working on the emotionality. Anxiety, the source of the reactivity, is the prime mover of the emotional forces.

People seek relief from anxiety. Humans are known to bind anxiety by finding scapegoats. Blame displacement tends to be focused on two functioning positions, regardless of who may be in those positions—namely, the most responsible and the most vulnerable. We look for parents, principals, priests, presidents, the police, and proper authorities to be our Dempsey dumpster. Or we find people who are in a vulnerable position, such as immigrants

(Mexicans and Muslims), strangers (homeless), the young (teen drivers), women (single working mothers), someone who is new, and even children. Either way, the persons in those positions become the receptacle of the emotional waste of others. Instead of seeing this as a matter of displacement, a leader acts like a victim who has been unfairly treated. In reality, it is part of the leadership process to be dumped on and blamed.

Anxiety, as neurobiologist Bruce McEwen contends, makes us "dumber." We lose the ability to imagine and think logically. So it is not only external challenges but equally internal ones that leaders will need to work through. A leader's own anxiety can put him or her in a mental straitjacket.

An army officer who trained both the special forces and the regular army noted that the Green Berets consistently outperformed the general infantry in survival school. In both cases, all the soldiers were hooded and shot at with blanks, deprived of sleep and food, and put through obstacle courses. The training officer said the special forces "don't get as stupid as fast as the rest under stress." This confirms Dr. Friedman's assertion that the number and strength of the stressors in the environment are not the determinative factor in dealing with troublesome circumstances. The key variable is the organism's response. With chronic reactions, wild things happen. Resistance and sabotage become fierce. But if there is a degree of calmness and thoughtfulness informing one's self-regulation, self-awareness becomes larger and more impactful.

As previously noted, Dr. Bowen gave the word *emotional* a specific meaning—anything in our behavior that is instinctive, automatic, and mindless. About 90 percent of our daily behavior is reflexive and impulsive. We share this characteristic with all creatures. Both *instinct* and *incite* share the same Latin root word, *instiguere*, meaning "to prick." Instincts are quick, sudden, and immediate. Before we can think or imagine, the pricking has happened. Security first, thought later. In the midst of confusion or threat, we say we have to "let the dust settle" or "the air clear" before we can engage in logical pursuits. With our emotional side in control, we are not open to reasonableness and insight. Yet it is our ability to think, observe, and ponder that distinguishes us from the rest of animate beings. We can go beyond our automatic impulses.

Alan Jacobs wrote *How to Think*, calling it a survival guide for a world at odds.[2] He tells a story about a person who becomes incredibly upset listening to a speaker with whom he disagrees. His revulsion intensifies with every new paragraph. When the speech concluded, the irritated listener approached the speaker and relayed his dissatisfaction. The speaker replied, "Give it five minutes." Wrought by emotion, the hearer had done all the thinking he was going to do. His quick visceral reaction (what someone calls the "race to the bottom of the brain stem") led to a snap judgment. Emotion doesn't waste time. And anxiety is one sure way to speed reaction. Speed can kill in emotional processes just as much as it may on a highway.

Police officers, a former Dallas police chief points out, exist "to protect the people of the city," but they are "also strongly guided by one of the primal urges that unites us as humans: survival." Brown writes in *Called to Rise* that with training and experience, reaction time changes. You still have the same physical reactions, but they slow down. "You're able to think more clearly, control your reflexes," Brown affirms, "and make smarter decisions."

In an emotional regression, the survival instinct turns into a whiplash, a jumped-to conclusion, or a quick fix. People are not thinking slowly enough to observe, deliberate, and respond. Calling everything you don't like "fake news," acting like a victim (injustice collectors), or distracting others from reality, you join the regression.

THE LEADER'S NOTEBOOK

The Big Six

Anxiety can be adaptive, prompting change. But its intensity and length lead to reactive behavior. Six major triggers of anxiety are noted in this chapter. Which ones are most prominent in your own system? Have you worked through one of the six? What happened? Are you "stuck" systemically because of one or two of the triggers? In the space provided, note on the left side anxiety that has been adaptive and on the right side the anxiety that led to reactivity.

Disruption	
Feeling trapped	
Threat	
Differences	
Uncertainty	
Depletion	

3

SOCIETAL EMOTIONAL PROCESS

I believe man is moving into crises of unparalleled propor-
tions, that the crises will be different from those he had
faced, that they will come with increasing frequency for
several decades. . . . Change will require a change in the
basic nature of man, and man's track record for that kind
of change has not been good.

—Murray Bowen

AMERICAN SOCIETY

Seeing parallels between familial and societal functioning, Murray Bowen added an eighth principle to his theory, namely "societal emotional process." All human systems undergo periods of regression or progression, depending on how well they adapt to the challenges of the time. For instance, historian Barbara Tuchman portrayed the calamitous fourteenth century as dealing with "galloping evils, pillage, plague, and taxes," which underscored tragic conflicts, an eradication of a third of Europe's population due to the Black Death, the Church becoming more worldly than spiritual, the hovering shadow of pestilence, and peddling influence with money. Then, "by some mysterious chemistry, energies were refreshed, ideas broke out of the mold of the Middle Ages into new realms," and society found itself on a new creative curve, bursting with artistic imagination, religious renewal, and fresh ideas—a renaissance.[1]

Bowen believed that American society had developed a regressive pattern after World War II, and it accelerated in the 1960s. With massive cultural shifts, the regression may yet produce more and more crises, testing the integrity and stamina of all leaders. Systemic change is slow and stubborn. Bowen even wondered if it would take a major crisis to shift the long-established patterns.

AN ANXIOUS SYSTEM

I worked with a hospital supported by a religious organization. For four years, it had tension between fulfilling its mission serving the health needs of all people and meeting the bottom line. The tension pulled parts of the health center in opposite directions. The CEO decided to leave, citing the intransigence of the people, their pettiness, and the persistent squabbling. The surgical unit that provided a large percentage of the income challenged the mental health department. Many users of the mental health unit paid on a sliding-fee scale, amounts that did not cover costs. Some saw the disparity as a financial detriment to the facility. But the mission statement would have been compromised if these services were curtailed or eliminated.

When people put the red pencil to work, the mental health center's costs relative to the overall operation was a financial drain. Complicating the matter, the mental health unit was the only facility of its kind within a radius of fifty miles, offering help to those with depression, addiction, and other psychological burdens. Closing the unit would be disastrous for the community at large. Looming in the background, too, stood the uncertainty of the national health care debate.

When it came to selecting a new administrative leader, the combating parties went to battle. The board had supporters on both sides. How could the staff and board come to an agreement about the role of the next CEO?

I was asked to work with them regarding the stalemate. I interviewed a sufficient number of people to identify the primary issues and locate the ongoing sources of strong emotionality. I chose motivated and mature people to serve on the action planning team, which would begin to address what we knew. I have learned that you cannot pour insight into unmotivated people and that immature people will shy away from controversies. We isolated the primary actions that the new CEO would have to process: (1) reduce the emotional aspects of the dilemma, (2) list realistic options, (3) inform employees of what had been happening, (4) appraise the financial situation by an objective source, (5) look to the immediate community and state for sources of additional funding, (6) set a timeline for completing the task, and (7) employ a new director who had experience with conflict.

I had to deal with those who sought immediate results, who were apt to fault others, and who could only think in a "cause-and-effect" manner. We agreed that to get beyond the crisis, blame was unacceptable, time would be needed to complete the process, and we would look for the mutually reinforcing factors that brew dissension. I noted that even if the mental health unit reduced its services and practiced a form of financial triage, the emotionality that had created and sustained the polarization might remain. I reinforced the idea that differences do not lead to harsh differing. Polarization is maintained by emotional energy.

We agreed on principles of operation. I introduced Dr. Edwin Friedman's schema of what happens when chronic anxiety infiltrates and migrates through a system. We would use the typology as a way to measure or gauge progress. Though a few objected to using a negative scale, others believed people could see the improvements better from the lower end to a higher one.

CHRONIC ANXIETY

I noted that we had to have a structured process because structure corrals anxiety. Surely, it does not end it. But the emotional bleeding ceases. When chronic anxiety goes unabated (this battle had a four-year duration), Friedman cited five reactions (to which I have added two) that keep things in place:

1. emotional reactivity replaces careful thought;
2. the herding instinct is strong (circle the wagons, strength in numbers, groupthink);
3. blame displacement (finding a scapegoat);

4. wanting a quick fix (for the reduction of unpleasant anxiety);
5. weakened leadership (failure to take a stand and disappoint some segment of the system);
6. secrecy (never on the side of growth or challenge); and
7. invasiveness (boundary violations).

A new CEO was appointed, Sister Georgina, to the satisfaction of most. She had a background of working with systems in similar difficult situations. She made it clear at the beginning that providing excellent health care was the first priority. She would not accept fault-finding. "Light a candle," she repeated; "do not curse the darkness." Fees at the mental health center had to be increased, but in dire cases minimal costs would be involved. The mental health center would write the new fee structure and policy statements, pending approval by a finance committee.

Sister Georgina embodied Bowen's statement about neutrality:

> A basic principle in this theoretical-therapeutic system is that the emotional problem between two people will resolve automatically if they can remain in contact with a third person who can remain free of the emotional field between them, while actually relating to each.[2]

Even though Sister Georgina made significant strides in changing the emotional climate, a few stormy characters sabotaged her, wanting to thwart the progress that was made and keep the inadequate emotional immaturity alive. I have found that sabotage usually arises and maintains itself when someone is losing power/control or not getting what they want from the process. And some people are "injustice collectors": nothing is ever fair, right, or proportionate.

THREAT

What I have described in the microcosm of a hospital can happen in a larger system. There is growing evidence that the emotional problems in society are similar to the emotional problems of a family, a small group, or a hospital that employs 125 people. When a system is subjected to chronic anxiety, people begin to lose contact with their principles, self-determined goals, and intellectual capacities. There is a behavioral regression, as well, such as blaming and demanding instant solutions. We are in a period of societal emotional regression wherein anxiety undermines our objectivity (fake news), sets up bogus enemies (white supremacy), denies tradition (custom-made reality), imports antiscience (climate change denial), lavishes attention on the weirdest image makers (conspirators), and magnifies differences (racial, immigrants).

The emotional forces observed in families occur in society at large. Lower levels of accepting responsibility for one's own emotional well-being are seen and accepted. Blaming is endemic. Patience is an alien trait. Certainty is demanded.

On the global scene, we see societal regression in religious wars, terrorism, ethnic cleansing, mass migration, nuclear threat, disparity in accessing resources, and the revised myth of the hero-warrior who will give bogus guarantees to the collective survival brain.

Bowen, foreseeing crises after crises, mentions that societal regression only subsides when anxiety lessens. If we could gain more control over our reactions to the reactivity of others, we could begin to take constructive action based on principle and thoughtfulness.

For an example, the *New York Times* op-ed writer David Brooks gave an account of societal emotional process in a column titled "Guns and the Soul of America." He claimed that people from the agricultural and industrial sections of America strongly feel that their way of life is being threatened by the urban elites in postindustrial society. Farms and factories are not the primary feeders of the economy, but even more, the "values" they represented have given way to new ones. The old markers of identity, such as self-reliance, individual freedom, patriotism, and control of one's destiny are no longer buttressing and informing the American identity. To restore the old distinctive tracks, these folks champion guns, flags, and legitimate citizenry.

When society is subjected to chronic, ongoing anxiety, it may lose the capacity to think imaginatively and resort to more and more emotionally determined behaviors. What Brooks describes is reminiscent of the time other changes had an effect on social groups. Weavers felt threatened by the new technology of automatic looms and threw their shoes (*sabot* = shoes; source of the word *sabotage*) into the newfangled instruments. Likewise, in

Holland, the shipbuilding guild protested the new ways of shipbuilding. In Switzerland, the printing press emotionally disturbed those who manually transcribed texts. Anxiety is ubiquitous.

NEURASTHENIA

Struggling with a long-standing bout of anxiety, Scott Stossel draws upon the travail of others in his revelatory book, *My Age of Anxiety.*[3] He mentions George Miller Beard, a young physician, who wrote an article in a medical journal around 1870, proposing a new American affliction—"neurasthenia"—which literally means "weak nerves." Its etiology was constant change mixed with a relentless drive for success and status that had no satiation point. Anxiety had become the alpha emotion in the United States. Its symptoms were insomnia, dizziness, dry skin, diarrhea, ringing in the ears, numbness, flatulence, hot flashes, tenderness in teeth and gums, itching, cramps, heart palpitations, and vulnerability to hay fever. The symptoms were so sweeping as to be senseless, sounding more like the litany of a hypochondriac than evidence of one illness.

With the disruptions of the Industrial Revolution and the expectations of new wealth in the Gilded Age, people had become unmoored from the values of the simple past of town and country. Still, as Stossel noted, we have no "magical anxiety meter" to offer objective analysis. What we know is that the survival of the organism is as old as the human race. We are capable of apprehending the future, of imagining what tomorrow might bring, and of looking ahead, and we have the capacity to worry excessively and to envision ominous events.

Stossel alludes to Rollo May's observation that meaninglessness was the real threat, the neurasthenia of the twenty-first century. The theologian Paul Tillich, responding to the disintegration he saw in Western Europe in the mid-1930s, referred to four contributing forces in "Storms of Our Times." First, he said a cloud of *"indefinite anxiety"* hung over the nations. Their institutions—economic, social, religious, and political—were floundering, and "everything was without foundation." Expecting a breakdown any moment, people longed for security. They were engaged with their survival brain, caught in imaginative gridlock.

Next, *uncertainty* rippled across Western Europe, leaving many searching for assurances at any price, even subjection to a powerful leader if necessary. In a warning to us now, Tillich remarks that a freedom that leads to anxiety has lost its value—we think, "better authority with security than freedom with fear." Third, Tillich named *loneliness*, which opened the door to despair, not a good situation for clearheaded thinking. Movements formed as much for community as for relevance. In conclusion, Tillich noted the rise of *meaninglessness*, foreshadowing fatigue and carelessness, a period of anguish with no assurance of a future. All four citations exposed people to the hero-warrior leader who would fill the vacuum with boastful promises—security, certainty, community, and new purpose—but lacking a soul.

Tillich's musings about the storms of his time should awaken us to the leader who will use whatever means to sway and galvanize the emotionally vulnerable. A feeling of "indefinite anxiety" alone could stimulate people to look for confectionary comfort, release from a turgid state of affairs, and a quick resolution for "weak nerves."

Sure, George Miller Beard exaggerated a cultural illness. But his exaggeration did not annul the potential of a societal emotional regression. Stossel himself reports that the World Health Organization found that Americans are four times more likely to suffer a generalized anxiety disorder than Mexicans. Moreover, Mexicans recover from the disorder twice as fast. When Mexicans immigrate to America, their anxiety soars. Who should be talking about building a wall?

THE LEADER'S NOTEBOOK

Chronic Anxiety's Effect on the Emotional Systems

As you scan the list below, where would chronic anxiety show itself in your system? Once you select one or two items, what is the antidote?

Reactivity	quick, instinctive, and mindless reactions to events, issues, and people
	little capacity to self-regulate
	defensiveness
	aggressive (arguing vociferously) or passive (sulking)
	negative diagnosing of others
Herding	circle the wagons
	groupthink
	insist on consensus
	desire for good feelings and harmony
	lack of decisiveness in order to avoid offending anyone
	stuck-togetherness
Blame displacement	fault others
	focus on pathology
	scolding, attacking, maligning with no reason
	pin responsibility outside of self
	lack of self-awareness
Quick fix	impatience
	low threshold for pain
	look for symptom relief rather than real change
	avoid challenge
	bypass messiness of emotional processes

Failure of nerve	leader panders to "noisy wheel"
	leader pleases, rescues, or enables
	leader abdicates role of taking first step (reads the polls, weighs the odds)
	leader is conflict avoider
	leader in name only
Secrecy	skews perceptions
	locks in pathology
	opposes healing and growth
Invasiveness	use of power to gain access
	brushes off limits, rules, or any defining line
	invader feels entitled; invaded feels shame, disgust, or other negative emotion
	give into impulsive needs at another's expense

II

THE LEADER'S PRESENCE

Bowen described a continual effort of working on himself to be a better leader in all his groups, whether family or work. His efforts on his own functioning positively affected the organizations he led. In this way, he learned that the ideas, so helpful to families, were actually useful to all groups (systems) of humans.

—Roberta Gilbert

I am what I am because of who we all are.

—Leymah Gbowee

The only way you can gain both a clearer view and some perspective on the bigger picture is by distancing yourself from the fray.

—Ron Heifetz

Quite simply, in any human group, the leader has maximal power to sway everyone's emotions.

—Daniel Goleman

4

HEADS UP!

AT ODDS

When you saw the refurbished building that housed the Frontier Real Estate office, you would have wondered how they made the ugly building into a usable space. The business started nine years ago as a "mom-and-pop" shop. Seth Goodman and Ashley Crane combined their talents and started a low-profile residential real estate enterprise. Seth was the "people" person, and Ashley served as the business administrator. Together, they formed a solid team. Expanding their services to commercial properties, Frontier grew steadily and employed fourteen full-time and six part-time people.

Trouble started to brew, however, when Ashley's son Todd joined the firm. Todd was a high school football star who injured his knee in college and had to end his aspirations for a professional career. After "sowing his oats" for a while, he returned home. Ashley put Todd in charge of a new real estate project, a business park. The affable optimist Seth, though wary of the appointment, agreed, with the provision that the work would be completed as planned since a large financial investment had been made. But Todd's inexperience, coupled with periods of arrogance, put the project behind schedule. Seth warned Ashley about the situation, but she defended her "flesh and blood."

When Seth finally asked Ashley to replace Todd, she balked and emotionally withdrew from Seth. A longtime relationship was in peril. Frustrated, Seth unilaterally removed Todd from the park project and replaced him with an experienced person. Ashley threatened Seth with a lawsuit. Recognizing the effect their behavior was having on others, Sergio Salinas, who had been a longtime employee, urged both of them to meet and deal with the tension, as they would often do. But for some reason Ashley interpreted Seth's action as a repudiation of her and as an insult to Todd. Nonetheless, Seth surprised everyone and sold his shares in the business to a regional development company, leaving Ashley to deal with the new officers and their team of attorneys. Meanwhile, Todd left town, like a rat abandoning a sinking ship.

Once the triangling started between the three, it spread to others; and now with the new partners, the old staff, and Ashley, the triangles formed and interlocked fiercely. Ashley took a lot of the burden on herself, to the point that her health deteriorated. By this time, Seth and his wife had moved near their daughter in another state. Bitter and feeling abandoned, Ashley had to sell her interest in the business.

Before he moved, I had a chance to speak to Seth, who had invited me to do a training for the staff several months before the tension erupted between him and Ashley. I introduced the Bowen family system theory to the staff. Seth was flabbergasted as to how emotionality could overtake a system, even after years of cooperation. He credited some of the trouble to himself, citing what he called his "unscrupulous optimism," a concept he had learned from C. S. Lewis. His high need for conformity and good cheer, he thought, had its drawback. His intuition told him Todd was a risk, but for the sake of pleasing Ashley and avoiding disagreement, he took the path of least resistance. Ashley, he thought, had to deal with her own contribution to the circumstances, being emotionally fused with her own son.

IT'S THAT LIZARD BRAIN AGAIN

The life of a lizard is simple. Lounging on a log, the lizard's tongue flicks at a crawling insect. The insect is gone. The lizard doesn't pause to think about whether it is lunchtime yet. There is no question about whether the insect is clean enough to devour. Lizards don't worry about calories or carbs. They don't lightly shake grains of salt on the insect or dip it into cocktail sauce. They just eat. The lizard has nothing to decide, nothing to remember, nothing to learn, nothing to be anxious about, nothing to prepare for. Instinct handles it all.

Many times, humans function at the instinctual level of a lizard. Nature has endowed all living creatures with very similar nervous systems. Deeply wired into the protoplasm of reptiles, mammals, and humans is a survival mechanism, a powerful drive for self-preservation. Whenever we sense that our life is at risk, whenever we imagine a threat, whenever we suddenly feel vulnerable—we react. It is automatic, reflexive, and mindless. Brains are designed to react to threats, not to meditate on them. When faced with a challenge to our well-being, rapid reactions take over.

Once the threat disappears, animals "shake off" the effects with twitching. Only humans develop long aftereffects. Worrying beyond reason, we can think of a terrifying "what if?" The frontal lobes (thinking) are put into service of the survival instincts. When you automatically rationalize to defend yourself, your reacting brain has put your thinking brain in its command. You imagine an inventory of horrible things. In her book *Fear and Other Unwanted Guests*, Harriet Lerner says she wishes she could be like her cat Felix, who feels fear only when fear is due. You can conjure up in your mind the worst things that can happen. You don't need lions, witches, or dark holes to frighten yourself.

Early in life we begin to distinguish what is strange and threatening from what is familiar and comforting. Friend or foe? Pain or pleasure? For us or against us? Recessed in the most primitive part of the brain lies the amygdala (*uh-MIG-da-la*), a cluster of cells the size of a grape. The amygdala serves as an early warning signal for danger, constantly scanning the environment for information about what might bring us harm, pain, or injury. Linked to the sensory system, it is ready to blast off an alarm to the brain stem that will set off the automatic reactions of fight, flight, or freeze. In *The Tending Instinct*, UCLA psychology professor Shelley Taylor notes that women often react to stress with an instinct to "tend and befriend." (Recall Greta taking her hand and reaching for Bert's.) Once the alarm is sounded, the body's stress-response system is activated, bringing changes in blood pressure, a rapid increase in heartbeat, and a quick release of hormones. The chameleon dashing across the driveway or the deer sprinting into the woods has an amygdala no different from our own. Going on danger alert, the amygdala sends a message to the motor centers of the brain. We jump, tremble, scream, run, stand still, or hold our breath.

The amygdala keeps us out of harm's way when there isn't time to think. Escape first, ask questions later. Since the amygdala promotes rapid processing of sensory data, its strength is quickness, not accuracy. It simply can't take time to deliberate and mull over the details of the moment. This primitive brain must operate in a yes-or-no fashion. It's this or that, safe or dangerous, one or the other. It also relies on generalizations and stereotypes to do its urgent and rapid work.

The amygdala has no sense of time. If a stimulus provokes the fear response early in life, that stimulus is registered in our memory bank. The event is circled and redlined. If the stimulus repeats itself later in life, the same reaction occurs.

SELF-PROTECTION

In studies of people whose amygdalae were active, researchers found that subjects' memory systems were affected in two ways: (1) less information about their immediate environment and what was happening was available to them, and (2) the pool of objects that resembled the original stimulus was much larger. Threat assessment deteriorates with the triggering of the amygdala. A minor comment is perceived as a major insult. Benign details suddenly take on an emotional urgency. Things are out of proportion. Perception is lopsided or truncated.

When we are flooded with anxiety, we can never hear what is said without distortion or respond with clarity. Bruce McEwen, a neuroendocrinologist, comments that stress limits our repertoire of responses. Fixated on what is endangering us, we forfeit our imaginative capacities. We act with a small and sometimes unproductive repertoire of behaviors. With fewer alternatives, we act foolishly. When the amygdala is in control, our perception warps measurably. Our mind is set in imaginative gridlock, we obsess about the threat, and our chances of changing our thinking are almost nonexistent. Reactive forces rule.

In a second study of police officers, paramedics, and combat veterans, researchers found them experiencing the horrible situations they faced in different ways. The greatest predictor of whether or not people developed symptoms as a result of their work was *how terrified* they were and *how long* they remained terrified. Intensity and duration were the key factors. If intense and prolonged, their amygdalae went uninhibited and unregulated. The researchers concluded that to assist frightened people, you want to calm them down. When they are in a more relaxed, receptive, and aware mode, they can respond less defensively. They shift from survival to growth, from protection to interpretation.

Anxiety is built into the nervous system for the sake of preserving the organism and the species. When the amygdala is removed from an animal or is damaged, the animal's behavior changes. Aggressive monkeys become passive. Likewise, mice will amble near cats with no fear. In the biblical book of Isaiah, the prophet refers to the peaceable kingdom where the lion and the lamb lie down next to each other—quite possible if their amygdalae are muted. Woody Allen quipped that nonetheless he thought the lion slept better than the lamb, referring to the powerful remembrance of the instinctive brain.

A NEURAL TUG OF WAR

Your anxiety system can make you too sensitive to danger, diminishing your mental judgments. If called upon too frequently, the body's capacity to adapt to pressure wears down many bodily systems. Under acute conditions, stress protects. But when chronically activated, anxiety can produce not only numbness in thinking but also disease.

On occasion the amygdala will take the "high road" rather than the "low road." Instead of sending signals to the brain stem for quick action, the amygdala directs its signal to the cortex, the thinking brain. The route of the high road provides us with the advantage of time. We can think and look for alternatives. Our thoughts are more precise, accurate, and clear. The cortical thinking brain will not rely on first impressions, act on impulse, or react instantaneously. With the thinking brain in charge, we can be intentional rather than instinctive, responsive instead of reflexive, adaptive rather than defensive, proactive instead of reactive. Of course, the potential always exists for a neural tug of war. The primitive and advanced systems can tussle to achieve control. We are caught between our prefrontal cortex trying to make sense of what is happening and our amygdala sending signals to arouse our emotions. In order for an organism to survive in the long term, it will eventually need contributions from the left prefrontal cortex so that thoughtful approaches rather than instinctive ones guide behavior and decisions. The low road has the advantage of speed and simplicity. The high road provides accuracy and precision.

William Shakespeare lyricized the whole brain as the "soul's frail dwelling-house." Now some neuroscientists locate sacredness precisely in the left lobes, which house the left prefrontal cortex. Paul McLean, another neuroscientist, refers to the left prefrontal cortex as "the angel lobe." Without the left prefrontal cortex, humans would function just like another animal, letting instinct handle life. A nightmare would ensue: creature pitted against creature in a struggle for survival.

The left prefrontal cortex houses our humanity. It is the brain region just behind the eyes that integrates information and inhibits emotional impulses that rise from the amygdala. The left prefrontal cortex is fully developed only in humans. It is crucial for all higher-order, purposeful behavior. Neuroscientist Alexander Luria has called this region of the brain "the organ of civilization." His student Elkhonon Goldberg has referred to it as the "executive brain." If it is impaired, we lose hindsight, insight, and foresight. We function with fewer social constraints. We express less responsible behavior. From medical history, we learn about the case of Phineas Gage—a promising young railroad foreman in Vermont, who, through a bizarre accident, had his left prefrontal cortex severely damaged. A responsible, mild-mannered, and sociable person, he was transformed into an irresponsible loudmouth and an irritable individual. His physician remarked, "Phineas Gage is no longer Phineas Gage."

As much as you need an active amygdala to warn you of danger, you likewise need the left prefrontal cortex to monitor it. Imagine the havoc we would encounter if the amygdala had no inhibitor of its alarm signals. With each anxious "beep," we would automatically assume the defensive position and react. We would be chronically anxious. The survival brain would be totally in charge of our lives. If anything threatened our viewpoints, we would instinctively reject it.

Early in my consulting work, I made the mistake of thinking that if I presented issues clearly, people would respond appropriately. What I discovered is that not all people in a given situation will find clarity comforting. Even if the information is quite clear, if it runs contrary to someone's viewpoint, they will contest it. Their own emotionality overrides their thinking capacity. Their emotionality limits the thinking brain's capacity to focus on the facts. The survival brain will protect you not only from bodily harm but also from challenges to your world of insight and meaning.

HUMAN MENTAL CAPACITIES

Healthy functioning of the left prefrontal cortex is the best hope for a sane and safe world. It is the organ that enables each of us to be a responsible and responsive person, to be self-aware and thoughtful of others. In the absence of the left prefrontal cortex, the amygdala romps around like a two-year-old, principles are not in place to guide behavior, and a sense of hope is lost.

The brain is an incredible instrument, but whether it is at the service of a chronically anxious person or a reflective person makes a world of difference. The prefrontal cortex enables you to function in five unique ways:

1. Humans can observe self and environment:

    - You can stand back from experience and be conscious of it.
    - You are self-reflective.
    - You learn from experience by studying yourself.
    - You can look inward to discover what is happening in the outside world (a dog knows a lot but doesn't know it knows a lot).

2. Humans can exercise social competence:

    - People can see beyond self.
    - People can see and regard the other person as a separate individual, not there simply to copulate with or to masticate.
    - People can choose to cooperate with one another (have you ever seen someone throw a bone to a pack of dogs, and one dog says to the others, "After you"?).

3. Humans can use imagination and think critically:

    - You can picture different scenarios.
    - You create possibilities.
    - Imagination develops options, drawing attention to the unusual.
    - You can weigh issues.
    - You can judge.
    - You use principles to guide behavior.
    - You employ meaning to modify innate tendencies.

4. Humans can regulate emotional forces:

    - You can quiet an excited amygdala.
    - You can consciously cool down reactive, impulsive forces.
    - You can veto or put brakes on instinctual reactions.
    - You can exercise self-control (a dog could never play poker with its tail wagging with each good hand).

5. Humans can project into the future:

- Humans are capable of predicting, planning, and setting a schedule.
- The left prefrontal cortex is the only part of the brain with a sense of the future.
- Animals stay in the instinctual moment, but humans can anticipate.
- A sense of the future endows humans with the capacity to find purpose and meaning in life.
- Without the capacity of the left prefrontal cortex, there would be no hope.

THE ASSOCIATING BRAIN

Another important aspect of the brain is what neuroscientist Elkhonon Goldberg notes in his book *The Wisdom Paradox*.[1] The two hemispheres of the brain interact with each other, but each one has a unique function. Goldberg's ideas about the hemispheres are not ones commonly thought of—that is, "left-brain" people are linear and logical while "right-brain" people are creative and disorderly. He says this is more poetry than science. He reports that individuals with right hemisphere dysfunction experience difficulty with the unknown: (they) "usually eschew novel situations. They tend to cling to routines and be rigid, fearful, and resentful of any departure from well-entrenched scripts in any life circumstances."

Goldberg's observation is corroborated by the experience of Kurt Goldstein, a neurologist who worked with right-brain injuries during World War II. His patients exhibited little capacity for imagination. They kept their closets in definite order. The patients placed their shoes and shirts in specific places. If their closets were disturbed, the patients panicked. The patients could not make a new arrangement or imagine a fresh order. Due to damage to the right lobe, they simply couldn't process new messages through the right brain.

When the right hemisphere processes new information, it stacks the information up against what is already known. To classify the new, our brains compare it to old recipes, known scripts, and familiar categories that are stored in the left lobe. The right lobe is always giving the left lobe something to think about. Over time, it is neurologically simple to become set in our thinking, especially if we are never exposed to something new. Some people seem to prefer specific rules for living that they can memorize and store in their left hemisphere, never having to hassle with ambiguity or uncertainties. Adaptive change involves stimulation of the right hemisphere. Complicating matters, the right hemisphere not only processes new information but also our negative emotions—like frustration, anxiety, and anger. Neurologically, we are designed to be skeptical or emotional about new things. Meanwhile, the left hemisphere is active with positive feelings such as love and joy. We like what we know.

You learn by building a library or archive of patterns—familiar faces, favorite foods, and core principles. Your ability to recognize a new object, a fresh face, or an unknown solution as a member of an already familiar class of objects or archival mental images helps you to bring more experience to bear on how you deal with the new. If in your "library of associations" in the left hemisphere no image or idea corresponds to your experience, anxiety can grow rapidly. How do you close the gap between your remembering self and your experiencing self? Do you become a lizard or a living soul?

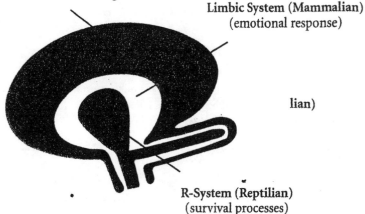

Neo-Cortex
(conscious rational thought)

Limbic System (Mammalian)
(emotional response)

lian)

R-System (Reptilian)
(survival processes)

Neo-Cortex (Thinking)	Limbic System (Feeling)	R-System (Reacting)
• attention	• connection	• automation
• mental problem solving	• regulating stable environment (blood pressure, tempera-ture, sugar level, immune system)	• sensory motor, physical processes (approach-avoid, fight-flight)
• many choices		
• organizing world		
• memory		• no choices
• thought-out be-havior	• very few choices	• preserving self
	• bonding with others	• safety
• source of values, beliefs, convictions	• play	• survival behavior
	• emotional behavior	• source of reactivity
• "light" shedding	• source of commu-nity	• "cold" acting
	• "warm" giving	

Peter Steinke

THE LEADER'S NOTEBOOK

Right to Left

Suppose you are a leader of a group of ten people and the group has for its purpose one of either the common good or personal profit. In each column, note what image or idea comes quickly to mind for either goal. Is there a difference in your responses when you read the listed word? Complete both columns.

	Group Goal = Common Good	Group Goal = Profit
	Image, Association, Idea	
participation		
artistic expression		
complexity		
story		
limitation		
advance		
transformation		
markets		
being relevant		
unilateral		

5

THE NON-ANXIOUS
PRESENCE

MIND AND MATTER

For a long time, people resisted the idea that mind could move matter, that attitudes could influence molecules, or that faith could play a part in body chemistry. New evidence supports the notion that confidence affects physiological processes, and a positive outlook impacts emotional states. A correlation exists between expectations and physical and emotional condition.

One study, for instance, investigated the influence of thinking on marching. Israeli soldiers were required to make a forced march. They were divided into four groups that were not allowed to communicate with one another. Each group went over the same area on the same day with the same backpack. Group 1 was told the exact distance they had to go (twenty-five miles) and were kept fully informed about how far they had traveled. Group 2 was not told how long the march would be and were not informed regarding the distance they had traveled. Instructed to cover twenty-five miles, Group 3 was told at the last moment that they were expected to march more miles. Meanwhile, Group 4 was told they had to go twice as far as the first group, but they were stopped about halfway there. They walked the same distance, but they walked with different ideas in their heads.

The effects of the march were measured in terms of morale, performance, and change in body chemistry, especially hormones that were believed to elevate as stress mounted. The results follow:

Group 1: least evidence of stress; highest degree of hopefulness
Group 2: fared the worst in all postmarch measurements
Group 3: a very discouraged lot
Group 4: high levels of stress and demoralization

The degree of physiological and psychological stress was determined more by what was in the head of the soldiers than in their tired feet.

If groups can be affected by marching orders—clear or confused—systems can be equally influenced by the steady and calm presence of their leadership. The leader's self-command can stabilize the whole system, despite the pervasive anxiety that infiltrates the community. In practice, the non-anxious presence of leaders has a positive effect. It leads to less friction, more imagination, and healthier functioning. How a person handles one's own anxiety, the anxiety focused on him by others, and the anxiety seeping into the system is vital. Leadership, often thought to be about action, is more about interaction—that is, regulation of a person's reactivity when relating to others. Since anxiety can be infectious, the leader does not want to be its source or its transmitter. In today's topsy-turvy emotional world, the leader cannot be as anxious as the people served. In effect, the overanxious leader leaves the system without real leadership.

The non-anxious presence is an anomaly, never a full-blown reality. It is intended to be a description of a way of being, the capacity to

- manage our own natural reactions;
- use knowledge to suppress impulses and control automatic reactions;
- keep calm for the purpose of reflection and conversation;
- observe what is happening, especially with oneself;
- tolerate high degrees of uncertainty, frustration, and pain; and
- maintain a clear sense of direction.

We have the dual capacity to act without thinking (reactivity) and to take time for thought before we act (response). We cannot, however, control original impulses, even their first impressions and expressions. Nature rules and follows its design. Act first, think later. Reactivity is necessary for survival. But we also have the potential to stop and think—and then act. Both reactivity and response have advantages. Reactivity's advantage is that there is no hesitation. Reactivity does the "quick and dirty" work. Response provides the advantage of time so we can think before acting. This, however, is extremely difficult amid stress and pressure. We feel an instinctive push for a fast relief of stress.

The non-anxious presence responds (exercises thoughtfulness) instead of reacting (a mindless action). Under conditions of extreme anxiety, most people become an anxious presence, lacking restraint and acting on impulse. The overexcited sympathetic nervous system causes the body to collapse and feelings to spill over the banks and flood the system. An adrenaline surge sweeps over the body. Once it floods the brain, our attention is focused solely on the outside threat. We concentrate narrowly on something and are unable to process other stimuli or to shift our attention. When obsessing about danger, our capacity to see or hear other information is nearly eliminated. However, the person who can more readily control anxiety is always more aware of its presence. To be a non-anxious presence means to acknowledge anxiety but not let it be the driver of behavior. Being aware of it, a non-anxious person says, "Anxiety is there. Yet, now that it is where I can see it, I can keep an eye on it. I won't let it slip back into unconsciousness. With anxiety up front in awareness, I can tame and harness it. While I may feel like pouncing on someone, I choose not to submit to my instincts. I have good access to my thinking facilities. My emotional state is not in overdrive. I will survive this; I can take the sting out of anxiety and be a calming agent."

With this kind of thinking, a leader brings more imaginative approaches to bear upon the system. The leader is not marooned in tunnel vision.

SELF-REGULATION

The influencing potential of the non-anxious presence is not to be confused with being "cool" or being "nice." Nor is it to be construed as denying anxiety in ourselves, as if unaffected by events. The non-anxious presence involves engagement, being there and taking the heat if need be, witnessing the pain and yet not fighting fire with fire. The non-anxious presence means we are aware of our own anxiety and the anxiety of others, but we will not let either determine our actions. Obviously this means that we have some capacity to tolerate pain both in ourselves and in others.

Reactivity "feeds" reactivity. When two parties are emotionally engaged, their defensive/survival mechanisms are in control. But instead of reinforcing reactivity, the non-anxious presence will be

- thoughtful before acting;
- calm and poised;
- self-aware;
- intentional about using "I statements";
- asking questions or reframing issues; and
- working on more chosen, deliberate responses.

MODERATING EFFECTS

In any emotional system, automatic forces will be strong. They are intended to be powerful. They provide safety and ensure survival. That's precisely why our reactions to any kind of threat are defensive. But we know that reactivity (defensiveness) will excite counterreactivity from other people. At some point, we have to make a non-anxious response to break the cycle.

John Gottman, who has done extensive research about why some marriages succeed and some falter, offers several helpful insights about human relationships. He found that couples, in both successful and nonsuccessful marriages, fall into the cycle of reactivity.[1] Their conversations become a volley of accusations. Before long, the conversation escalates into a blazing argument. The difference, however, between the couples who remain together and the ones who separate is that the successful couples stop the cycled argumentation sooner—that is, before it erupts into complete loss of self-control. The nonsuccessful couples get wrapped up in their own automatic reactions to one another and keep the vicious cycle going. Of course, we know that it isn't only couples who engage in these contentious quarrels. Given sufficient anxiety, people in any relationship can allow automatic forces to rule the day.

Gottman has also learned in his research that how a conversation begins can determine how it ends. If a conversation starts harshly, chances are high that reactivity will conclude it. The harsh startup sparks strong emotionality, which is often difficult to turn down or turn off. Leaders, of all people, need to see what part self plays in automatic reactions and control their part. It takes a disciplined effort to manage self: to step back for the moment, observe clearly, select a response, act on principle, and keep a course of direction.

WHAT ICE WANTS, ICE GETS

Sir Ernest Shackleton epitomizes the concept of the non-anxious presence. Shackleton, an early twentieth-century explorer, led an expedition to complete the first overland crossing of Antarctica. Setting sail on the ship *Endurance* on December 5, 1914, twenty-eight men took the risk to battle some of nature's harshest conditions. The crew suffered unbearable situations almost the entire 634 days they were gone. They had no communication with the rest of the world. Whether they were dead or alive, no one knew. They endured brutal cold and ice. At times their hunger touched the borders of starvation. Then, 327 days into the expedition, the *Endurance*, squeezed between huge blocks of ice, was crushed. Frank Worsley, the captain of the ship, noted in his diary, "We had lost our home in that universe of ice. We had been cast out into a whole wilderness that might indeed prove to be our tomb."

The men saved what they could from the ship to survive. Soon they were confronting not only the forces of a hard environment but also their own human nature—boredom, paranoia, physical exhaustion, and other manifestations of psychological weariness. According to Worsley, their leader, Sir Shackleton, exhibited a "calm, confident, and reassuring" presence. Its effect? In his diary, Worsley wrote two citations about Shackleton's presence and its impact on the group: the "leader's state of mind is naturally reflected in the whole party" and "had effects on the attitudes and behaviors of the troops." Sitting on a small piece of ice, buffeted by piercing wind and threatened by chunks of colliding ice, Shackleton himself remembered his feelings: "I confess I felt the burden of responsibility sit heavily on my shoulders; but on the other hand, I was stimulated and cheered by the attitude of the men"—the cross-pollinating effect of the non-anxious presence. Miraculously, all of the members of the expedition survived. The non-anxious leader can broadly affect the entire emotional field. It's as if the leader's calm, reflective demeanor becomes an antibiotic warding off the toxicity of reactive behavior.

THE LEADER'S NOTEBOOK

Mind Mapping

Mind mapping uses the mind's design of axons to discover associations between ideas. Fill in words or phrases that come to mind when you see the phrase "non-anxious presence." Share responses with others.

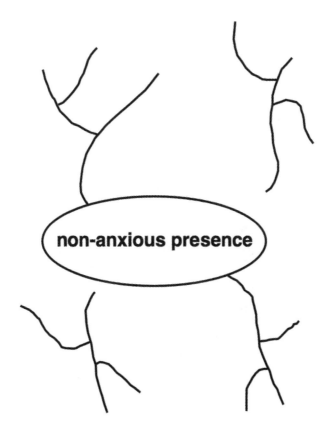

6

IMPACTING THE
EMOTIONAL SYSTEM

BRENT'S DILEMMA

A mutual friend suggested that Brent call me. I was the director of a counseling center when he called, assuring me he was not "crazy." But, he added, he was confused and worried. I assured him that craziness was not a prerequisite for coming to the center.

Brent owned a small company that manufactured leisure furniture, mostly for summer and outside use. When his father died suddenly, Brent had to take the reins of the company at the age of thirty-six. After college, Brent worked there for three years in sales. He left to become sales manager at a decorative lighting company. In his newly inherited position, Brent simplified things by dividing the company into three units—administrative control, design and production, and sales. Each unit had ten to twelve workers.

"When I divided the workforce into three divisions, each group wanted my attention. I thought I had given birth to three children. The tension has steadily risen. Mary, who started with my father twenty-three years ago, feels entitled. Dominic in sales dislikes her. He says she is too bossy. Some of the employees are taking sides."

"What have you done?"

"Avoidance."

"And you wonder why they squabble?"

"I'm a salesman, not a CEO."

"Really?"

"Sales are different. You go your own way. You dance to your own music. At the top, you have to listen to a lot of music."

"You have a steep learning curve."

"Am I hopeless?"

"If you want to be."

We exchanged more details, and before he left I gave him an assignment: return with three written solutions to the problem.

When he came the second time, I listened to his first two suggestions, which were weak. But his third idea was brilliant. He would place 15 percent of the annual profits into a workers' bonus pool. Each person would have to be responsible for their individual goals and also the goals of the whole system. He would put Mary, Dominic, and Vincent (design and production) in charge of goal achievement. If both goals were accomplished, bonuses would be distributed. Strangely, the strength of the emotional process involving Mary and Dominic lessened but arose in a new dyad, between those accomplishing their goals and those lagging behind.

CALM

crisis

CHANGE | new situation

Leader's Being and Functioning

bewilderment | FOCUS

stagnancy

CHALLENGE

Peter Steinke

During the next several sessions, Brent realized that no one in an emotional system is better positioned to influence outcomes than the leader. How he handled himself was far more impactful than any know-how or tool of persuasion. We explored the three ways that happens: positive outcomes emerge if the leader's presence and functioning are centered in principle, based on self-regulation, and anchored by thoughtful positions. Principle provides clarity, self-regulation helps to avoid extremes, and thoughtful positions lead to necessary action.

CRISIS/CALM

In times of crisis, a system functions best when its key leaders regulate their anxiety. The crisis certainly ushers in confusion, as well as a temporary period of powerlessness and hopelessness. It is a crucial time for the community to slow down and reflect on what has happened. The natural instinct is just the opposite—to press immediately for decisions, explanations, and actions to dispel the awful uncertainty and helplessness. Impatience has its source in anxiety. Being hasty is low-road functioning.

During a crisis, a structure of some sort is needed. When things are falling to pieces, the emotional system needs a container—something to hold the parts together, something that promises that chaos is not king. Crisis may shatter our beliefs, threaten our security, and expose our vulnerabilities. To counteract these and other disturbing consequences, leaders, by their patience, hope, and reframing the event, can calm the people who are affected.

BEWILDERMENT/FOCUS

Systems that lack a focus are like a sailor on a lake without a destination. With no port in mind, the sailor will not know how to adjust the sails to guide course. The sailboat will drift or meander. The system, not focused on its mission (destination), wanders or floats aimlessly too.

You may have heard the story depicting three bricklayers working on the same project: The first bricklayer is asked what he is doing. His answer: "I am laying bricks." The second one replies that he is erecting a wall. The third bricklayer says, "I am building a cathedral." In bewildering times, leaders need the third bricklayer's vision: focusing on what might be possible and seeing the opportunity buried in the confusion.

"Not only are we entering a millennium of perpetual novelty, but also the future promises a continuous escalation in the rate of change," the late Rabbi Edwin Friedman observed. "The change will have a significant effect on the emotional processes of all families and other institutions." Friedman foresaw these circumstances creating a chronically anxious state for the immature members of society and a condition of permanent stress for all leaders.

Sometimes leaders get into the position of thinking they are primarily responsible for preserving tranquility. The last thing they want to do is upset anyone. Consequently, they hide embarrassing information, or they avoid making changes that might spark controversy. The leadership position favors "togetherness forces"—that is, the leader feels responsible for keeping the system together, for everyone's happiness and comfort. Anything that might jostle or jar the equilibrium is rejected.

STAGNANCY/CHALLENGE

In the Biosphere in Arizona, a three-acre greenhouse in the desert, people noticed that the fruit was falling off the trees prematurely. What had happened? Inside this encapsulated environment, wind, a force that challenges the trees' branches and strengthens them, is absent. Without wind, the branches do not gain sufficient strength to hold the fruit to the time of maturation.

The leader can most influence the system by challenging it. The leader functions like the wind. When challenging, leaders will surely kick up the dust of anxiety, since resistance is a natural reaction to challenge. Resisters essentially say, "Let us be content in our homeostatic world." A leader has to expect opposition when the community is resting comfortably, and then it is pushed, pulled, or stretched.

The leader challenges, but mostly at a rate people can absorb. Readiness needs to be considered carefully. Some challenges fail because the opportune time has not really emerged or the challenge did not enroll a sufficient number of people to support its implementation. If driven not by someone's impulsiveness but by urgency, the challenge gains support or momentum.

Opportune times to challenge usually appear when

- the community hits bottom;
- real events open eyes and sharpen awareness;
- a sudden, shattering experience occurs; or
- the system is in a learning mode and someone capitalizes on it.

NEW SITUATIONS/CHANGE

Western society is experiencing a shift from one historic period to another. No parallel exists in history with the current rate of change. What shaped past centuries is yielding to a fresh set of ideas and perspectives. For thousands of years, civilizations focused on continuity. The overriding and new fact of history is living with constant, radical change. Rapid transformation is becoming a normal way of life.

Having worked with different kinds of systems involving change, my most salient observations include the following:

- Change is an emotional process.
- Change is resisted less if it is associated with mission (this is who we are, what we are about).
- Some change is slow (it takes over fifty years to grow almond trees); some change is swift (radishes grow in three months).
- Identifying the "early adopters" enhances the chances for change because most are late adopters (cf. Everett Rogers, *The Diffusion of Innovations*).
- Seldom, if ever, does change happen because at first a majority votes for it.
- John Kottler believes that a sense of urgency needs to accompany plans for changing anything significant.
- And Kottler, in his book *Leading Change*, tells the story of Don, who purchases his first house in New York, a dwelling that is over six decades old, fitting the category of a "fixer-upper." The realtor reminds Don to make a list of what needs to be done and do it immediately. But Don says he is broke; he will do it gradually. Five years later, he found

the realtor's words to be true. He never got to do the changes. Homeo-stasis (same position, same state) is strong.

- Change would be easy if it were not for emotionality. But that's why we have leaders.

THE DOWNSIDE

Since leaders more than anyone can influence the emotional system, they can do it negatively, too.

"I'll take care of you . . .
    so you don't have to hear harsh things."
    so you don't have to struggle with making a decision."

"I'll keep the lid on the pressure that threatens to boil over . . .
    so you are not forced to think."
    so you are not emotionally upset."

Friedman noted that when a leader is predominantly a "peace monger," a "failure of nerve" follows. The leader concentrates on consensus and harmony. But the system's togetherness forces will turn against a leader if the choice is between following the leader or losing their tranquility. Note Friedman's warning:

> The chronically anxious, herding family will be far more willing to risk los-ing its leadership than to lose those who disturb their togetherness with their immature responses. . . . It endeavors to accommodate the disruptions of the immature.[1]

Friedman believed that the antagonism of the anxious is proportionate to the niceness of the leader.

If the leader adapts his functioning to the weakest members, he enables their dependency, encourages their happy ignorance, and reinforces their helplessness. To protect a system from bad news or upsetting changes is to admit that the system is weak and fragile, too brittle to be challenged. The threshold for pain is low, and the opportunity for changing is negligible.

Distress is not always an obstacle to learning. Pain can be a teacher. Real learning begins when the threat of pain emerges. Everyone has *learning anxiety* (a general dread of entering unfamiliar territory or exploring new ways of understanding). The anxiety that spurs growth is *survival anxiety*, when you choose something new because survival itself is at stake.

If the leader does not have some degree of toleration of pain, it is doubtful that others will be able to tolerate pain and use it for growth. As a result, Friedman asserted, the weakest, most dependent, and most emotionally driven people will control the system. They will influence the emotional field, not you.

CHALLENGE

Survival leaders are safety focused. "The safest place for ships is in the harbor," Edwin Friedman wrote, "but that's not why ships were built."

Challenge leaders are not intimidated by the unknown or unpredictable.

Challenge Leaders	Survival Leaders
Take thoughtful action.	Take expedient action based on emotional pressures.
Risk goodwill for the sake of truth.	Play it safe for the benefit of preserving stability.
Stay the course (hold steady).	Use quick fixes for restoring harmony.
Manage self.	Attend to those who look outside of self for rescuing.

CONNECTIONS

To be a leader, one does not have to have a major title, a bloodline, a pedigree, or vast experience. Willie Jefferson will not make the Leader's Hall of Fame. For one thing, he is only twelve years old, and he's mixed race, with a black father and a Eurasian mother. Willie had the advantage of being tall and older looking for his age. Some might say he was aggressive, but in truth

Willie was assertive. At his church, Brother Smithers (the pastor of the small church) distributed one-hundred-dollar bills to ten people, including Willie, and asked them to invest the money in some project to double or triple the original amount. The money raised would be given to "Sack It to Them," a food distribution project in the area for children who would otherwise face hunger if not for filling their backpacks with food on weekends.

Another program I know is called "Love for Lunch," where four thousand children are fed during periods when school is not in session. Three years ago, in its infancy, 150 children were fed. From our earliest days, we are nurtured by food, and the formula "food equals love" is etched in our minds. In ancient times, we have learned, one did not attack one's enemy at mealtime; and now, we know the adage that the "way to a man's heart is through his stomach." The very word *companion* (closely associated with *community*) is hewn of *cum* and *pane*, signifying sharing bread.

Having endured intermittent periods of hunger, Willie knew better than most the necessity of food. He formed a group composed of other young people and a few adults called Foodheads. They made cupcakes for sale at local events; they learned how to make a beehive, stings and all, and marketed honey. Once a month, they sponsored at a local pizza store a meal of bread and water, charging two dollars. One month, Willie would invite the high school football coaches and players; the following month, all the clergy in town, and then the mayor and his entourage. "Foodheads" drew the attention of the press, and soon its impact spread; but in so doing, it became too big for Willie and his peers to handle.

Willie's story is compelling, but it was not without setbacks and adversities. No doubt, his youthfulness played into his enthusiasm and his naivety. But what sealed the effort for him, as it would for anyone, was his ability to *stay connected* to others. Some people thought he was too misguided or the pawn of some liberal politician or clergyperson. But differentiation, carefully considered, is the ability to define oneself (caring for others) and remain in contact, which is as much a survival mechanism as any self-defense measure.

Regarded as one of the most popular bloggers in the world, Seth Godin has shared his insights in print, like his book *Tribes: We Need You to Lead Us*:

The easiest thing is to react.
> The second easiest thing is to respond.
> But the hardest thing is to initiate.
Reacting is intuitive and instinctive . . .
Responding is . . . thoughtful action.
> But both pale in comparison to initiative.
> Initiating is really and truly difficult, and that's what leaders do.[2]

The next step is yours if you want to lead, come crisis, change, challenge, or focus.

THE LEADER'S NOTEBOOK

The Roundtable

Working with systems, I like to assemble the leaders for a thinking session. In groups of three or four, the leaders discuss one of the statements in each of the three sections. If time allows, the group will proceed to other statements.

Crisis/Calm	*Stagnancy/Challenge*
• In the event of a crisis, take your own pulse first. • A shift in functioning of one person will shift the functioning of others. • Calming down is essential but only as a first step in (removing) anxiety; the next step is thinking.	• Challenge is always on the side of healing and growth. • Risk is an inconvenient necessity. • Ships are safest in harbor, but that's not why we have ships. • Put an ice cube in a hot cup of coffee, and the heat moves from the coffee to the ice; there's movement because there's challenge.
New Situations/Change	*Bewilderment/Focus*
• Our brain is much better at changing the world than living with the change. • If you don't like change, you'll like irrelevance less. • No emotional system will change unless people in the system change how they function with one another. • Systems that avoid conflict are also very likely to resist change.	• Having a focus mobilizes people's energy. • Turn off autopilot and pay attention. • There are no shortcuts to any place worth going. • What happens when we have no maps, no copies, no landmarks? We walk in circles.

THE LEADER'S
FUNCTIONING

For whenever a "family" is driven by anxiety, what will also always be present is a failure of nerve among its leaders.

—Edwin Friedman

What astonishes me, no matter how often I see it, is the power with which strong negative emotions can trump cool thinking.

—Walter Mischel

Robert Sapolsky explains that our stress-response system, like that of all mammals, evolved to react to brief and acute stresses. . . . But modern humanity has no contest with lion attacks. Instead, most of our stress today comes from mental processes, from worrying about things.

—Paul Tough

The best leaders are the best learners.

—James Kouzes and Barney Dosier

The biological building blocks we share with bacteria, plants, sponges, worms, bees, fish, frogs, dinosaurs, rats, mice, cats, monkeys, and chimps make it possible for us to survive, but we are ultimately made more than mere survival machines. Although we live in the present, we humans live for the future.

7

THE BALANCING ACT

NEWTON'S WORLD

Isaac Newton believed that atoms were the smallest bits of matter. They were conceived to be solid, impenetrable elements. Each atom occupied its own space. No atom could get inside another atom; no atom could be reduced to anything smaller. He also contended that all atoms obeyed the same laws. Newton's world was fixed and predictable.

Newton's atomistic model extended beyond physics. It became a paradigm for thinking about society. Individuals were considered to be the atoms of society, and immutable principles and institutions were the means to keep the separate parts intact. Using Newtonian concepts, Freud explained his psychology of relationship. Every person is isolated and impenetrable (unknowable). No one can know another person, but each projects something of him- or herself onto the other.

Western medicine has thought atomistically, breaking life into small, isolated parts. Physicians regard the body as a collection of separate elements. Medical specialists will attend to one body part or section. Several correctives to this way of thinking have emerged. Immunology, once thought to be a system unto itself, is now referred to as *psychoneuroimmunology*, the interaction between brain, other bodily systems, and the immune response. Also, in treating patients, physicians have begun to pay attention to their own behavior and the patient's sensitivity as part of the treatment process. Addressing physicians, Norman Cousins, who wrote about overcoming a serious illness through the therapy of humor and laughter, urged that when they entered the patient's room to remember that the main distance is not from the door to the bed but from the physician's eyes to the patient's. "That distance is best traveled when you bend low to the patient's fear of loneliness and pain and the overwhelming sense of mortality that comes flooding out of the unknown, and when your hand on the patient's shoulder or arm is a shelter against darkness." Cousins envisions the patient to be a "penetrable" person, someone who can be affected by the physician's touch and presence.

Western education followed the Newtonian approach, dividing knowledge into discrete parts (reading, writing, and arithmetic). Schools taught "subjects" and had "departments." Students would major in a special field to become expert in one part of knowledge—nutrition, mechanics, optics. Interdisciplinary studies are still rare. Business, too, broke production into assembly lines. Companies structured themselves into subdivisions for sales, research, finance, and production.

About one hundred years ago, quantum physics emerged as the primary model of the physical world. Only recently has it spread into some common ways of thinking. Quantum physics is about the behavior of subatomic particles. Quantum physics, in contrast to Newton's physics, contends that there is no world composed of solid, individual parts unaffected by and unrelated to others. There are no lonesome leptons.

EMOTIONAL FUSION AND CUTOFF

One can be an individual only in a relationship, and a relationship can function properly only when individuals play distinctive roles in it. Parker Palmer, in *The Courage to Teach*, summarizes differentiation as embracing "the profoundly opposite truths that my sense of self is deeply dependent on others dancing with me and that I still have a self when no one wants to dance."

Individuality forces are derived from the need to be centered, to have a mind of our own, and to grow as an emotionally separate human being. Togetherness forces are derivatives of the need to mingle, to be close, to exchange warmth, and to participate in the life of the other. Optimum functioning as a leader would require balancing the two forces, with neither force overriding the other. To live a healthy life requires the capacity to stand apart and to stand together. Sometimes the balance is difficult to achieve because the forces are at odds. The two needs are difficult to meet at the same time. Both of these are very sensitive to anxiety. Such sensitivity may create an imbalance, pushing or pulling a leader to an extreme. Leaders must thread the difficult passage between standing too far away from their followers or blending in too much.

A Loss of Balance

If anxiety about being separate is intense, a person gets too close or too entangled with others. This is *emotional fusion*. If a person's anxiety about being close is intense, he or she gets too disengaged or too remote from others. This is *emotional cutoff*.

Emotional Fusion

Fusion is a word borrowed from physics. It describes what happens when metals are melted together. At certain temperatures, the metals lose their properties, and they cannot be distinguished one from the other. Emotional fusion happens when people lose their "self." It occurs when one person dominates and the other dissolves into subservience or when both are "nice" to one another to tighten their bond or when each one functions to take care of the other person's feelings. Rainer Maria Rilke described a "fused, muddy communion" as being composed of two "unclarified, unfinished, and still incoherent" people.

Systems are uniquely vulnerable to fusion, particularly if it is an idealistic group. When premium value is placed on harmony, acceptance, and belonging, people resist information that might disturb their peace. No one wants to speak the truth. If people are emotionally linked, they may not have sufficient space to challenge one another.

"In any anxiety field," Bowen remarks, "the group moves toward more togetherness to relieve the anxiety." More togetherness, however, can distort people's ability to discern and judge. James Surowiecki, author of *The Wisdom of Crowds*, contends that "the more influence group members have on each other, and the more contact they have with each other, the more likely they will believe the same thing and make the same mistakes." Vested in compatibility or likeness, systems can easily reject differences or information that contradicts their experience. They fear anything that might drive the group apart or alienate someone.

If the community's cohesiveness is strong, their sharing of moods, their behavioral patterns, and even their hot buttons will be alike. It is important to note the difference between giving up self in fusion and giving up self for cooperation or for the community's welfare. Fusion results from *automatic* reactions. Cooperation is *chosen*.

Emotional Cutoff

Rather than standing out from others (differentiation), a person may stand outside of their circle (cutoff). Genuine separateness is differentiation within a relationship, not independence of it. Cutoff is an exaggeration of the need to be separate—"I can only count on myself," or, "I'll do it alone." Again, the difference between people who cut off and those who take strong positions is in their functioning. Cutoff is reactive. It's an automatic defense. In contrast, a well-defined stance is chosen, thought through, and clearly expressed. With cutoff, a person attempts to gain a sense of identity *over against* another person. By projecting a negative label on another ("girlie man," "geek," "chicken hawk"), the person seeks to gain a positive identity for him- or herself. A person defines self against another. Self-definition does not come from one's own center of being. To continue the position of "againstness," the emotional distancer often becomes dogmatic, opinionated, and doctrinaire. Omniscience means no one can give you anything. You have it all.

It is wise to remember that whenever someone cuts off from someone significant in their life, anxiety continues, but the awareness of it diminishes. The anxiety not resolved in one relationship tends to be acted out in another one unknowingly.

MATURE FUNCTIONING

Differentiation

At times, you may choose to pull back from others or to give in to them. But it is intentional, chosen behavior—not automatic. Cutoff or fusion can be troubling behaviors when they are instinctive—that is, emotionally driven. And, as we know, it is easier to change a habit than an instinct.

The ideal way of functioning in Bowen theory is through the process of differentiating, the balancing of the two emotional needs of separateness and closeness. Expressing separateness, a person defines self to the other (I think, I hope, I know). The other person may be threatened, uninterested, or emotionally upset. The mature person stays connected with that individual. A less mature person would withdraw (distance) or insist that you change (fusion).

In differentiating, it is beneficial to regulate your anxiety and keep your focus on your goal. An excellent illustration of differentiating behavior comes from a story told about Abraham Lincoln. Running for Congress, Lincoln learned that his opponent, the Methodist evangelist Peter Cartwright, was coming to his area to conduct a revival. Lincoln thought this would be an opportunity to hear what his rival was saying. At the revival, Cartwright asked all those who wanted to go to heaven to stand. Many did. Then he asked those who did not want to go to hell to stand. Everyone did, except for Lincoln. Seeing this as a time to embarrass his opponent, Cartwright said, "And Mr. Lincoln, where are you going?" Lincoln stood up and mentioned that he had come to listen respectfully to Cartwright. He was not prepared to answer either of Cartwright's questions. "But now, I would like to answer the question as to where I am going. I am going to Congress."

In another situation, I was coaching the leader of a nonprofit organization who had received a barrage of complaints from a group of volunteers who objected to his change in policy and staff. Some of the dissidents left. One of the organizers, however, chose to stay. After a period of cooling off, Henry, the antagonist, wrote a letter to Chad, the president, in which he mentioned that the last few months had been harsh. Henry wanted to take Chad out to dinner as a sign of reconciliation. But Chad's emotional bruises had not fully healed. He answered the request with this brief letter: "Thank you for the invitation. When I am ready for dinner, I will let you know." Chad defined himself and stayed connected, controlled his anxiety, and stayed focused on his work, being another Lincoln.

Helpful in this discussion, too, is the research of Walter Mischel. Working with preschoolers, the researchers challenged the children. They had the choice of eating the marshmallow placed before them or waiting twenty minutes so they could have two marshmallows. The researchers recorded the results and followed the children as they got older. At ages twenty-seven to thirty-two, those who had waited longer had a better sense of self, lower body mass, followed their goals effectively, and coped more efficiently with stress and frustration. Brain scans revealed that the low delay group had characteristics linked to addictions and obesity. Obviously the capacity to self-regulate and pursue goals led to better physical, relational, and psychological health. Who is your marshmallow?

HEIDI'S STORY

I was invited to start a community-based counseling center for a large urban hospital. After establishing seven satellite offices, I remained at the hospital and often received referrals from chaplains, nurses, and physicians. I remember one person quite vividly because of her differentiating capacities. Heidi Martin was from Germany and had married an American serviceman. For twenty-one years, they were childless but socially connected with many friends. Jim Martin came to the hospital for heart surgery but did not survive. Heidi was crushed. The hospital chaplain suggested that Heidi call for an appointment for therapy. A week after burying Jim, Heidi came to see me. She was emotionally adrift, but I sensed that she was a strong person.

The early months were typical sessions. But then she came expressing disbelief and a bit of anger. Several of her friends chided her for not emptying out Jim's room and donating his clothing and tools to charity. "I'm not ready to let go," she pleaded, "and I need time." More disturbing, she came a month later and reported that a close friend wanted to arrange a blind date for her. "I have had only five months to grieve, and they want me to return to normal," she gasped, "and they say I am way past normal in the process.

Am I crazy?" I explained to her that her friends needed her to be the strong, consistent Heidi they had known before Jim's death.

About the ninth month, I saw Heidi begin to heal. She said that she was thinking of reburying Jim in Illinois. She had buried him in Kentucky, near her sister, where she planned to retire in a few years from the position of vice president of a metal distributing company. "Pete, if I dig Jim up and bring him to Illinois, is this crazy or what? In two years, I will move to Kentucky, and dig him up again and return him to Kentucky." She started to laugh, calling herself *dumkopf*. You could see that her therapy was coming to a close. "And I know what Jim will be thinking. 'What are you doing, Heidi?'"

Heidi's leadership at work had always been stellar. Those around her needed her to be the Heidi they always knew. But she did not succumb to their neediness and did not sever ties when they shamed her for not relinquishing Jim's possessions. She defined her principle: "When I'm ready, I will dispense with Jim's belongings." Though she was anxiously distraught over their attempts to cure her quickly, Heidi stayed focused on her healing, adjusting to her time framework. Grief is not an emotional period in which to be calm and thoughtful, but the mature person takes the time to let things process and transform one's life.

THE LEADER'S NOTEBOOK

Undifferentiation/Differentiation Contrast

Crucial to the balancing act is a person's capacity to think clearly, observe, reflect on situations, and base choices and behaviors on principles. The behavior of the poorly defined and the highly anxious person is automatic, emotion driven, and based in the pressure of the moment.

Undifferentiation (instinctive, reactive, defensive, thoughtless behavior)

1. *Accommodates, pleases, or acts to take care of others' pain.* To maintain a relationship, the leader "gives in" and "gives up" self; is anxious about losing the approval of others.
2. *Focuses outside of self.* To stay close to others, the leader pays attention to the actions and feelings of others, not his own. How someone else will react is more important than how he can take a position.
3. *Connects emotionally.* To sustain a relationship, the leader reacts to anything that might disrupt or threaten it.
4. *Sets vague, nebulous goals.* To have a direction depends on the moment. The climate and goals change with events and moods.
5. *Seeks security.* To feel safe, the leader acts cautiously so as not to upset anyone.

Differentiation (intentional, responsive, responsible, thoughtful behavior)

1. *Takes a stand.* The leader works on self-definition based on values; knowing what he believes, the leader takes positions.
2. *Focuses on self.* The leader can see how she contributes to a situation; being self-aware, the leader makes changes in her own behavior and has the capacity to step back and see her own interactions with others.
3. *Stays connected to others.* The leader relates to others by listening, exchanging ideas, and working toward goals; greater capacity for cooperation and altruism.
4. *Sets clear goals.* The leader knows where he is headed; not sabotaged by others' reactivity because he lives with a purpose in mind, stays on course.

5. *Seeks challenge.* The leader seeks adventure; she knows that tension stretches a person's growth and stimulates the imagination.

Undifferentiation (Extreme Position)	Differentiation of Self (Balance of Two Needs)		Undifferentiation (Extreme Position)
Cutting Off	Defining Self	Touching Others	Clutching Others
reactive	intentional	respectful	reactive
automatic	chosen	playful	automatic
emotionally driven	objectively aware	emotionally expressive	emotionally driven
dependent	responsible for self	responsive to others	dependent
aggressive or defensive about keeping distance	self-directed action	trusting exchange	aggressive or defensive about embeddedness
unaware of own need for self	aware of self	aware of others	unaware of own need for self-expression
stiff, rigid boundaries	flexible boundaries (able to reinstate after loosening them)	boundaries lost in spontaneity, self-forgetfulness	soft, porous boundaries
overfunctioning to achieve self-sufficiency	functioning for self	allowing others to function for themselves	overfunctioning to achieve togetherness
minimal support, feedback, or encouragement from others	self-respect	respect for others, allows others to be themselves	forces others to be like self or allows others to force oneself to be like them
difference gained over/against others	defines self from within	defines self to others	differences are unacceptable; relationship defined by sameness
narrow goals	clearly defined goals for self	clearly defined relationship goals	vague, nebulous goals

8

AT THE EDGE

Let there be space in your togetherness.

—Kahlil Gibran

LOOSE ENDS

Rumors were rampant. Seldom did an employee leave Ross Distributors. When Paul Estancia resigned suddenly, others were surprised and baffled. No cause or reason stood out, and information was sparse. In the absence of information, a few conjectured as to why he left so unexpectedly, but they were as in the dark as everyone else.

With his two sons and daughter, Dane started the company, and he hired many friends and relatives as the business expanded. Outgoing and generous, he offered good salaries and bonuses. When a new financial officer from outside the circle of friends and relatives came, he discovered employee malfeasance in terms of charging personal items to the company credit card and overinflating the number of hours worked to receive double hourly pay. Only one employee was forced to leave; the others were to repay the excess amounts. Of course, no one paid much attention to the reimbursements to the company, a continuance of past neglect.

The real dilemma developed two years later when Paul Estancia left, followed by Wilbur Ross, a relative of the founder. Both had supervisory positions and had access to employee records. Disliking several people, both supervisors violated state labor laws and altered the employment files of the disfavored employees, substituting false and negative reports. With bogus documentation, Paul and Wilbur fired those with whom they harbored grudges. The ex-employees filed suit, and the subterfuge was discovered.

Dane had to admit that the company could no longer operate like a family business, with friendships intact and protected and structures loosely organized. Detail work was not Dane's forte. He had to hire assistants to institute lines of responsibility, work rules, and other boundary issues—and someone to oversee it all.

Ross Distributors is a microcosm of what happens in the absence or re-laxation of effective borders. People take advantage of loopholes and permeable parameters, crashing through or stepping over an approved marker, a person's dignity, or a social norm. I have yet to work with a system that did not have a boundary issue, whether it was about space, time, governance, relationships, authority, finances, or expectations.

By definition, a pathogen is invasive. Physically, a pathogen attacks living cells; likewise, pathogenic forces can interrupt the functioning of an organization. Unfortunately, the invasiveness is often enabled by others who remain silent about abuse, make excuses for the violation, or simply look the other way. It's systemic.

STARK REALITY

In the notorious case of Olympian physician Larry Nassar, more than 150 young female Olympians were sexually violated. The emotional system failed them, some fearing the loss of friends or jeopardizing their financial security if they reported anything. For some, truth got caught in their throat. Their conscience took a peek at what was happening and said to itself, "Just this one time won't matter." But it did for far too many, who suffered physical assault, mental torment, and brittle feelings of shame.

For almost thirty years, incredibly, accomplices let his pattern of behavior continue without anyone ringing a bell—until one brave woman would no longer conspire to be mute. And then, when she did reveal the violations, some labeled her an "ambulance chaser" and a "money grabber." Making matters worse, the victims were blamed—what woman would not like it?—so "it" is done in a clandestine way and excused.

Sexual abuse is a monumental default in leadership. Whoever they may be, some leaders will not deal with the emotional forces that lie behind the grabbing or stroking of nonconsensual contact. They silently lend aid to the perpetrators. They are essentially fused emotionally; they wear different clothes but have the same dead soul.

Boundary maintenance is a leadership responsibility. If the leaders themselves are perpetrators or accomplices to the action, the system is corrupt. If leaders challenge the pathogenic forces, they can expect pushback, since once a pattern is formed, its modification is resisted. It takes courage to call into question intrusiveness that is harmful, even if doing so is necessary.

In a time of Uproar, boundary violations increase as everything else is "up in the air" and "loose on the ground." In recent years, we have seen an increase in many forms of pathogenic activity, from suicide to bullying, from sexual harassment to bank overcharges, from fake news to reactionary litigation, from mindless partisanship to racial intransigence, and from money laundering to mass shootings.

BORDERS, LINES, AND EDGES

I find the belligerence with which creationists and evolutionary theorists debate the biblical creation story a waste of energy. I don't think the Hebrew writer of Genesis, or the readers, were drawn into the questions of creation's "how" and "how long." The Hebrews were more interested, it seems to me, in relationships that eventually culminated in the Covenant. The creation text itself is contained in the Old Covenant, and its great moral code, the Ten Commandments, addresses the connection between the divine and the human, and relationships between one another. In fact, the ensuing biblical stories center around the tension between two brothers; family squabbles; welcoming the stranger; the Jewish idea of distributive justice; being sensitive to the plight of the marginal, especially orphans and widows who had no social standing; multiple stories about the violation of personal boundaries;

and seeking shalom (the full flourishing of life) for all. Simply put, relationships count. That's the central narrative.

The key to it all, surprisingly, is the text of Genesis 1:2: "The earth was a formless void and darkness covered the face of the earth." It was an undifferentiated mess (or, to use Bowen's phrase, an "undifferentiated mass"), a maelstrom of universal proportion. The great fear was a relapse to the primal condition, a return to boundaryless chaos. The separation of the day from the night, the earth from the sky, and the land from the sea signaled the need for boundaries to ensure a relatively stable form of life.

Also, Adam was assigned to language arts class. Name it all! There had to be definitions. Literary critic Roland Barthes says the "founding function of differences . . . is the basis of language." Words provide distinctions, specificity. Without borders, there would be a gross "stuck-togetherness," nothing to hit against, no moving against the tide, no self/other dimension, no ordering function, no integrity, and a paralyzing sameness. Always, the latent threat of "a formless void" would linger.

Boundaries offer identification, protection, and connection. Writing about human nature, Theodore Schwenk says, "Boundaries are the birthplace of living things." Membranes encapsulate. "When the earth came alive," Lewis Thomas claims, "it began constructing its own membrane, for the purpose of editing out the sun." It is the membrane around a cell in biology, the skin of a raindrop, and the image of a separate self that provide identity and differentiation. Clouds have no membrane and, unstable, drift into other forms or dissipate into fog. Clouds develop types (cumulus, cirrus, and stratus) but not identifiable forms.

Besides identification, boundaries supply protection, particularly in nature. A tree is covered with bark to safeguard against insects, disease, and fierce weather; the atmosphere of the earth is a boundary that shields it from the sun's ultraviolet rays. The body's skin is a protective sheath.

Immunity protects against pathogens that exist under the skin, distinguishing what is self and what is not self. Immunity is a boundary protector. Pathogens, whether viruses, political dictators, unruly teenagers, sexual predators, bullies, terrorists, manipulators, gossipers, or Ponzi schemers, all invade the space of others. Immunity limits their pathogenic advantage. "Disease usually results from the inconclusive negotiations for symbiosis, an overstepping of the line by one side or the other," Lewis Thomas observes,

"a biologic misinterpretation of borders." Equally, the body politic needs the immune function to keep one person from folding into another or, in Bowen's terms, emotional fusion, a sticky-togetherness.

The body's immune function is a corporate intelligence; it recognizes patterns of foreign proteins and other harmful substances and resists. In a system, the immune function begins with the system's values and meanings. Who are we? What do we esteem? As a body becomes ill because of harmful agents, so too an organization or society can fragment and break down. One of leadership's primary roles, though seldom realized, is providing an immune response to irresponsible actions, unwanted attacks, or an aggravating invasion that is unwarranted. Absent immunity, pathogens romp around like uninhibited children.

Last, a boundary suggests the possibility of a relationship, pointing to the site where energy, matter, and information are exchanged. The genius of nature is its design for holding separate yet integrated components together. A philosopher said that "solitude is OK, but you need someone to tell you it is fine." Organisms die slowly without the capacity to metabolize, infants fail to thrive in the absence of touch and social interaction, and muscles atrophy when immobile. People without close bonds have earlier disease, greater severity of colds, more severe forms of depression and anxiety, and a greater risk for heart disease. Prisoners go berserk in solitary confinement. Isolation can be as harmful as obesity, poor nutrition, and lack of exercise. Heart specialist James Lynch asserted that companionship is the best form of life insurance. Relationships count!

CELLS TELL A STORY

Cell biologist Bruce Lipton says cells are "miniature humans." We share basic behavioral patterns with our own cells. Cells can learn and create memory. Once assigned a specific task, a cell becomes differentiated. It matures. Healthy cells interact with other differentiated cells. Essentially, we are a cooperative community of fifty trillion single-celled citizens. Together, our cells have the primary tasks of protection and growth. But they cannot operate the functions simultaneously; either you function to protect or to grow the organism. "The longer you stay in protection," Lipton notes, "the more you compromise your growth." Similarly with the body politic: if it stays in the survival mode, its growth is compromised. Individually, we have dual needs in our differentiating process—being separate and being close.

The cell is the basic unit of life. The word *cell* derives from the Latin word *cellelae*, signifying "a small room." A cell has walls, partitions, and dividers. The cell membrane creates a boundary where exchanges of energy, matter, and information are mediated.

As a cell matures, we say it has differentiated, meaning it limits its responses to a single task. The cell specializes, becoming bone, skin, or muscle. Each cell cooperates with other cells to create an entity much larger than itself (organelle, organ, organism, organization). Basically, the human organism is a society of individual cells cooperating with one another, reflecting separate yet connected components, the parts drawing close to one another, yet individual cells (selves) retain their integrity.

At a conference I attended, physician Sidney Baker asked, "Can you think of any pathology that does not involve a loss of integrity of a surface or boundary?" Pathogenesis (the invasion of infectious material) begins when the virus becomes aggressive. Lacking the equipment to replicate on their own, viruses need help from elsewhere. Targeting certain tissue, a virus fuses with the cell's membrane or burrows its way through the membrane. The resulting infection depends upon the interaction between the surfaces of the virus and the host cell. With infectious disease, the virus and the host cell become chummy. To complete the infectious cycle, a virus becomes completely dependent on the cell it attacks. Having gained entrance, a virus manipulates the host cell, running off copies of itself. For the moment, the host cell provides shelter and nourishment. Looking at the process from the point of view of the pathogen, what makes it happy or satisfied is a good meal. It is not far-fetched to see a connection between the virus having a good meal and an invasive person gaining control of another person by bullying or sexual harassment.

"It takes a membrane," Thomas noted, "to make sense of disorder in biology." The same is true in the physical environment. A river without

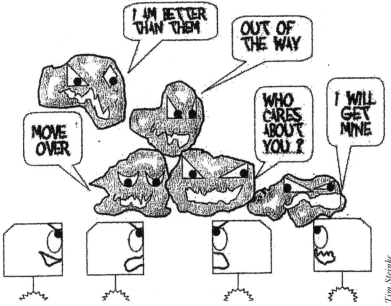

Tim Steinke

banks or a lake without borders creates a flood. A street without white and yellow lines creates dangerous road conditions. A society without laws devolves into recklessness.

Is boundary training the solution? I am dubious about the effectiveness of training that is data saturated. Most of these events rely on data and information, not building maturity. "Whether it is medicine or management," Dr. Friedman claimed, "it is precisely the omission of emotional variables that turns most collections of data into junkyards," and further, limiting the deluge of data will not solve the problem. "Only by adding emotional variables," he continues, "can people be led to more responsible positions for their responses."

People, Friedman believes, become addicted to data and resort to instant solutions for emotional relief, thinking less. They depend on the instinctive, automatic, reactive, lizard, non-thinking lower brain that is utterly vulnerable to anxiety. But this brain has never had a lesson and is not educable. It can snuff out, distort, and put on hold indefinitely any data someone offers if a person is not ready to hear it. In fact, Friedman called the internet the new "skid row." Imbibing data is nothing less than substance abuse. And we know what addiction does to behavior—keeping the dial of denial and deceit in the "on" position.

Data did not assist Katherine Dodge in her predicament at work. Married, a mother of two children, mild mannered, principled, and a cooperative soul, Katherine was also an exemplary employee, a chemist, who often collaborated with others on significant research projects. On her desk was a framed quote by Martin Luther King Jr.: "Our lives begin to end the day we become silent about things that matter." On the wall, she hung a small banner with the inscription "Free yourself," a quote by Rosa Parks. These were reminders from her days in college when she worked on a couple of student writer projects.

One day she took the words to heart and action. Katherine registered a complaint with the human resources department about the antagonism of a male coworker who doted on her appearance and his desires. Giving little credibility to her complaint, the head of the department said she had misread his actions. The person involved had a stellar career at the company. With no consequences for his behavior, the individual had no reason to change his approach to her. Her second appeal drew more attention, and the result was a company-wide reminder that certain behaviors were inappropriate in the workplace—again, data.

Undaunted, Katherine sent an email to two dozen employees, inviting them to a lunch meeting to discuss sexual harassment:

> Fake realities create a fake humanity. And a fake humanity generates fake relationships.
> If you have been the object of fake behavior, please attend our luncheon meeting.
> Sexual harassment is a reality here, but is being sucked into a dark hole of silence.
> Half the people here suffer from some degree of vertigo.

When the human resources staff learned about the email, they reprimanded Katherine. Her responsibility was to be a chemist, not the guardian of people's behavior. Nonetheless, fourteen women and three men met for lunch and decided to write a petition. As events transpired, the group discovered that the HR department's slow response was in part due to the fact that the vice president of the division was a classic offender. Katherine's group had what change theorist John Kottler called "a sense of urgency," fueled in part by their emotional needs. They would not capitulate to the delay tactics and let it all go. "Free yourself!"

It is helpful to remember that anxious, reactive individuals function in a way similar to viruses—neither have boundaries or respect the boundaries of others. Consequently, they go where they don't belong. They must have it their way, and they never learn from their experience. Self-regulation is a chore beyond their ability, perhaps even their consciousness.

THE IMMUNE SYSTEM

Leaders are pivotal in creating and maintaining boundaries. They are the immune system of the organization. When reactive people run roughshod over established courses of conduct, do irrational things, and cease reflecting on the consequences of their behavior, weak leaders will offer bromides of "we'll look into that" with no such intention. In reality, they cannot muster courage to express dismay or take corrective measures. They simply go along to get along. To lead, you frequently have to take the first step. You go out on a limb. Today, however, we have many leaders in name but not practice. Politicos want to be reelected; business leaders obsess about the bottom line. Leaders in religious institutions soft-pedal their remarks. Principals, parents, and other common leader types take the path of least resistance. It happens everywhere, but in the case of violating another person, the stakes are higher.

Boundaries by themselves guarantee nothing. People daily rely on their emotional (automatic) side to work through the challenges of the day. More than any one of us wants to admit, we spend 90 percent of our twenty-four-hour day functioning mindlessly. Delays, cover-ups, intrusions, co-opting (being co-opted), making excuses for defaults, deflecting responsibility, and other defenses (and offenses) come naturally. Why would boundary tension be different? Without principles, as Bowen insisted, we leave a lot of room for instinct to govern our lives. Subtract self-awareness, along with the absence of principle, and the choice to shift to awakened and intentional behavior is impossible.

Many like to say that boundary violators such as sexual predators or harassers function in order to have control of or power over someone else. It's not so much about lust, horniness, or sexual desire. I'm not sure it is as clear-cut as we make it; even more, manipulators and seducers mix in entitlement, no fear of consequences or retribution, and beliefs about their position of importance to embolden their crude and boorish behavior. Which, in Bowen theory, means that boundary intruders lack principle, self-control, and self/other distinction. It is more than a reach for power; it is human weakness on display in the disguise of power. If children engaged in similar behavior, we wouldn't assign it to power. We'd call it for what it is—immaturity.

Why is this important to the leader? First, a system cannot rise above the maturity of its leaders. Therefore, if the leader is lacking in maturity and tolerates the same deficiency in others, the most dependent, recalcitrant, and irresponsible individuals will be the de facto heads of the system. They will call the shots.

Second, the more regressed the system is, the less able it will be to get with the leadership it needs. The system will match its own immaturity, basically what's on the mind of the survival brain. So now we have political leaders that toe the line, conform to a formula, or sell their birthright to the highest bidders. We may want to call it politics as usual, but in reality it is sheer immaturity. We know that politicians shave the truth, fudge their positions, and offer rotten promises as ripe fruit. Still, we take it. That's the way it is. Certainly we exhibit our own immaturity in the process.

When was the last time you served the immunity function?

CHAPTER 8

THE LEADERSHIP NOTEBOOK

Leadership and Immunity

Dr. Edwin Friedman offers thought-provoking ideas in *A Failure of Nerve*. Listed below are direct quotes or statements summarizing his ideas. Which of the statements do you agree with, and which ones do you oppose? Is there a comment you would modify?

- The thinking processes that produce a failure of nerve and a quick-fix mentality in contemporary America are the result of a decline in maturity in an anxiously regressed society (p. 129).
- What is coming out of the top part of the brain (the cortex) is being driven by much deeper processes that emanate from the instinctive, nonthinking, automatically reactive reptilian part of the brain that is so vulnerable to surrounding anxiety (p. 130).
- Leaders are both overwhelmed and seduced by data when their own level of maturity in decision making, relating to others, and understanding situations is more critical than the data.
- Whatever drives people to drink drives people to data. Could the "fix" on data in American society lead to denial of emotional processes in how people function?
- Emotions do not simply modify thinking, reasoning, or decision making; they are part and parcel of the process of thinking (p. 117).
- The body is a systemic process whereby body parts impact one another. The Greek word *hormone* means *impact*. Since the brain has the most nerve connections, it releases the most "impacting agents"; it is a chemical cornucopia. In the body politic, the "head" (leader) is the one most impactful person. Brain and body work together. How, then, can the head find its way to be present in the body politic? In Friedman's view, the leader's presence will show up and impact the system through self-definition, self-regulation, nonreactivity, and the capacity to remain connected. It has little to do with messages, knowledge, data, and information and everything to do with impact through presence (pp. 124–27).

9

THE PEOPLE
OF THE CHARM

Narcissism is a disease of relationship, a disease that springs from a failure to make meaningful relationship to oneself and others. Its opposite is an attitude towards life that stresses the importance of commitment, involvement, love, sacrifice.

—Danah Zohar

THE PATTERN OF BEHAVIOR

For many, the retirement of Wade Simmons couldn't have come sooner. After serving as rector of All Angels Episcopal Church for twenty-three years, Wade's departure coincided with a loss in membership of young families. In haste, the vestry put together a search committee before Wade left. The leadership was ready for a fresh start. A list of four candidates was assembled, and interviews were set for each one. Pierce Ralston was the second person interviewed, and he impressed the committee so significantly that they canceled the remaining two interviews. Rev. Ralston would be the candidate presented to the church. Unfortunately, the rush to a decision left the vetting process unfinished.

Pierce came with high expectations and a sense of excitement. He did not disappoint many in the first six months, accumulating strong advocates during this early period. Parents of a seventeen-year-old daughter, however, came to the senior and junior wardens reporting Pierce's inappropriate advances with their daughter. Both believed the young girl had misread Pierce's behavior and that the parents had exaggerated the situation. The family withdrew from the congregation. Several comments from others about the same circumstances went unheeded.

An elderly woman in the congregation donated $200,000 for an improved sound system and other designated improvements. Pierce instructed the financial gatekeepers to use the money for a television setup so that Pierce's sermons could be seen and heard countywide. When the donor complained about the misuse of the designated funds, Pierce said she had trouble understanding church practices and had caused problems for previous rectors. A couple of members of the vestry questioned Pierce about the situation, but he lied to them, saying she had stated that he could use the gift for any purpose. This brouhaha came on the heels of Rev. Ralston's firing of a long-term staff person, whom he scorned and vilified. Actually, the staff person was confronting Pierce about his veracity. In turn, the veteran individual was released under the veil of having disturbed the entire staff.

There is more to this story of dissembling, blaming, and silencing others. Pierce's narcissistic behavior, especially the lying and the attacking of others, continued. Ministry, as well as sales, politics, and entertainment, are perfect venues for this type of functioning. While others point to narcissism as a character disorder, I see it as a system problem. Like Pierce, a person projects a sense of invulnerability and self-confidence. Many do it with charm. Nonetheless, the individual needs "narcissistic supplies," a reflection of one's grandiosity. If you do that, you will be given all the toys to play with that you would like. On the other hand, if you hesitate to do the mirroring, you are shunned, berated, marinated in acid remarks, or terminated.

NARCISSISM: A SYSTEMIC PROBLEM

Forty years ago, Christopher Lasch wrote about a developing way of life in the United States, narcissistic functioning (*The Culture of Narcissism*). "The new narcissist," Lasch asserted, "is haunted not by guilt but by anxiety." A hollow, weak, and superficial sense of self is covered with a veneer of glorious glitter. To protect one's shaky identity, the individual pretends to be self-sufficient and is anxious to the point of fighting off anyone's exposure of the masking. Part of the defense will be the devaluation of others, a vengeance against those who threaten the false scheme, and an automatic use of lies, misinformation, or exaggeration as protective shields.

Self-absorbed, the person lives with a "subjective experience of emptiness." Consequently, one engages in sexual permissiveness, restless desire, and an inability to suffer criticism. Compounding the situation, the narcissist has an impoverishment of intellectual curiosity. Illusion has to keep the impairment together.

The one who functions narcissistically cannot live without an adoring audience. Often they are people who are looking for the restoration of a Golden Age. The old order is littered with broken promises, and these people take the promises seriously. We have had front-row seats observing this. If you probe the list of narcissistic behaviors below, you will see that President Donald Trump is a master artist, and his admirers are model enablers.

I have worked with sixteen systems where the leader had strong narcissistic tendencies. Always, relationships were affected and polarization (which is emotionally maintained) ensued. One group sees the behaviors as destructive and the others are rabid supporters of the "sleeping giant" that returns to restore the kingdom to its glory. Invariably, the latter make excuses for the crude and cruel actions or decisions of the narcissist. They need the bloated bravado to stay puffed up as much as the one who projects it.

Narcissistic functioning is a systemic problem. People who function in narcissistic ways require others' admiration. Likewise, those who supply the admiration need the certainty and flattery of the admired because he or she is special. The system is composed of two needy parts, each dependent on the other. This system exists where a self-absorbed and charming leader becomes the object of others' devotion. You have a charmer and the charmed.

THE INVENTORY

The term *narcissist* derives from the Greek myth of Narcissus. A young man named Narcissus is followed by a lovely mountain nymph, Echo, who is hopelessly in love with him. Calling to his companions, Narcissus shouts, "Let us come together here." Echo responds with the same words and rushes to embrace her love. But Narcissus frees himself from her grappling and runs away. He cries out, "I will die before you will ever be with me."

Echo is devastated. In addition to Narcissus's rejection of her, the gods, for a number of reasons, punish Echo. They leave her only a voice and condemn her to wander in oceans and valleys. Spurned, Echo seeks revenge. She asks the gods to punish Narcissus, making him the victim of unrequited love. So condemned, Narcissus falls in love with his own image in a pool and pines away because he can never possess it. Unable to pull himself away from the contemplation of his own beauty, he starves to death, falls into the water, and is never seen again. Narcissus's tragic flaw is that he can never love anyone else. His love of self inhibits coupling, fertility, and the giving of self.

The narcissist must be given to. Psychiatrist James Masterson says, "The narcissist is motivated by the continuous need for 'supplies' to feed this grandiose conception of himself." The narcissist functions to maintain a projected, inflated image of self. By coercing, charming, or controlling others, the narcissist ensures that the need for supplies will be satisfied. Functioning to mirror his grandiosity, others guarantee him a sense of specialness, exaggerated importance, and superiority.

Some narcissism is normal, even healthy. Without it, no one could develop self-esteem or pursue unique ambitions. In contrast, pathological narcissism involves "excessive investment in self at the expense of investment in others." The list below highlights the ways in which narcissistic functioning is unhealthy:

- The person is endlessly needy, wanting repetitive approval. He is overly dependent on external admiration and hungry for continuous narcissistic supplies, seeking mirroring from others to back up his grandiosity.

- The person feels entitled to special consideration and is self-important (often exhibitionistic or dramatic to prove it).

- The person is capable of seeing only his or her own perspective, is intolerant of disagreement, doesn't discuss ideas but imposes them, is single-minded, believes in his or her own superior wisdom, and doesn't need help from others.

- The person is ruthless toward those who do not reflect back his projected image of specialness. Being vindictive, vengeful, devaluing, and abrasive, the self-absorbed publicly humiliates others.

- The person is prone to lying and is an expert at disguise.

- The person possesses little ability to control desires and lacks restraint, being impulsive and brash.

- The person displays an air of affability and self-confidence, appearing to be in command of situations, speaks with certainty, and has an aura of authority.

- The person presents him- or herself impressively. He is clever, charming, seductive, persuasive, and self-assured.

- The person shows no remorse, has thick skin and a rigid front, denies weakness, and turns around something that fails or goes wrong, blaming circumstances on others or claiming innocence.

- The person is often likeable and impressive, exhibiting so-called star quality, and can be fun to be with.

- The person is articulate and offers inspiring speeches that uplift people. He believes words can move mountains.

- The person is intoxicated by numbers, often distorting them to spice self-importance.

- The person is more interested in being admired than loved.

- The person is unable to use self-examination, is too self-engrossed to be self-observant, and does not fundamentally change.

- The person is obsessive about appearance (clothes, car, job position or title, location of residence, size of office space), well connected, and carefully selects and enlists others to buttress his or her swollen sense of importance. If male, he may have a "trophy wife."
- The person is ambitious to the point of being exploitative, making the environment resonate to his or her own needs.
- The person reacts explosively if his "false front" (projected image) is questioned or exposed. Perceived threats can trigger rage. Shame is totally avoided.
- The person is competitive, even to the point of finding enemies who aren't there.

THE EMOTIONAL EXCHANGE

Psychiatrist James Masterson notes that narcissistic functioning is actually the outcome of low self-esteem. It is a defense against insecurity and abandonment. Outwardly vain, the narcissist is inwardly impaired. "The narcissist resembles a psychological turtle with a hard, impenetrable shell," Masterson concludes, but it has "an equally soft, fearful center." The narcissist is not as certain as he or she looks, as evidenced by his or her supersensitivity to criticism. The illusion of stability is sustained by appearance. The narcissist is a master at denying reality, projecting an image of invincibility or charisma, and coercing the world to refuel his specialness. There is no transparency in narcissist functioning. It's all varnish and veneer—with lots of charm.

The functioning of the charmer and the charmed is one of mutual reinforcement—and self-deception. Neither one wants to know the truth. A person needs to be special, and a group of people feeds the specialness. One radiates glory and others bask in that person's glow. One projects an image of self-confidence, and the second party idealizes the person who can be so certain, so self-assured. Each needs the other. Their relationship is one of emotional fusion, for neither is able to stand back and see what is happening. The dynamics of narcissism revolve around the lack of self-knowledge. One person remains intoxicated with all the praise and adulation he manipulates from others, and the others are enthralled to be associated with someone larger than life.

Those who function narcissistically function well so long as they have people who adore them. But some can be so insecure inside that they must ensure their specialness with more and more admirers. They thrive on the ecstasy of numbers. The narcissist functions like a magnet, possessing the power of attraction. People caught in the spell surrender obediently. Under the spell of enchantment, they become dedicated followers as impervious to reason and truth as infatuated lovers. Many of the disciples of narcissists are vulnerable, lonely, and searching souls who mistake the narcissist's charm, self-confidence, and certainty for substance, when in reality it is pretentious fluff and feathers.

In the circle of charm, there are no checks and balances. Groupthink develops. Bowen called it "stuck-togetherness." Not surprising, many narcissistic leaders shield their swooning constituency from outside influences. They demonize outsiders who might potentially uncover the truth of things or expose the charismatic figure. In the circle of charm, the lights glare, but they don't reveal.

Those who are most vulnerable to charm are those people or groups who need stimulation outside themselves. Often they are depressed or demoralized. Many are looking for a high, some brightness or good feeling in their lives, to make them special. Masterson calls them "closet narcissists." Instead of investing their own specialness in a grandiose self, they invest in an omnipotent other. By associating with the special person, they get dusted with the same magic and importance.

Masterson tells the story of twelve individuals who called him for therapy. The calls came immediately after Masterson had been quoted in the *New York Times* about the major symptoms of narcissism. Each of the twelve came to him for an evaluation. Each indeed exhibited the very symptoms Masterson had noted in the newspaper article. All wanted to continue therapy, but Masterson did not have time to see them. He referred them to associates. None returned for treatment. Masterson saw this as just another symptom of their narcissism. They wanted to use Masterson as a narcissistic supply rather than seek help. Because of Masterson's reputation, being in therapy with him would greatly reinforce their special images of themselves, while being in therapy with someone else would not supply them with grandiosity.

Bent on being successful, the narcissist seeks out people who can contribute to that end. The narcissist needs the limelight. Others must play supporting roles. Many narcissists are workaholics who overwork their staffs and demand devotion from office workers. In return, the staff members receive full praise for their work. Many staff, over a period of time, begin to see through the empty praise and the false facade of concern for supporters. They realize that they are valued only insofar as they reinforce the narcissist's own glory. They are mere suppliers. But staff members need to be careful not to expose the sham. The narcissist works hard at eliminating feelings of shame. Shame involves exposure. Any shattering of the projected image of self-importance endangers the reinforcing grandiosity supply. The narcissist will lash out in rage against the whistleblower.

THE BLIND LEADING THE BLIND

When people are emotionally interlocked through charm, grandiosity, and need, they have insufficient distance to see what is really happening. Charisma is in the eyes of the beholder. To idealize someone as infinitely wise, incredibly kind, or unbelievably powerful can make a person feel safe. The admirer becomes childlike, diminishing self in order to gain from the magnification of the charmer. The narcissist and the narcissistic supplier form a system out of two impaired selves.

The need to appear larger than life and the need to believe in the super-specialness of others may provide solace and comfort in a threatening world. But it also limits authenticity and intimacy. Impaired selves create a false reality. If the circle of charm fails, charisma will be seen for what it is—a cheap substitute for differentiated living.

Any system can be a warehouse of narcissistic supplies. When each side feeds the other for years, allowing emotional need to glue them together, neither side will easily let the other go. Since narcissism is incurable, expectations that the exhibitionist/dramatic functioning will change are misplaced. Even the needy admirers seem unchangeable.

We have been witnessing a strong measure of narcissistic functioning in the presidency of Donald Trump. When someone has to use hyperbole to magnify achievements, exaggerate numbers beyond reality, and boost self-importance at the expense of others, the person displays a weakness, an immaturity, and a low sense of self. If these behaviors were true of our children, we would be worried about their level of self-esteem, no less their mental states.

I don't know what might lead to Trump's undoing, but if my experience with sixteen leaders who exhibited strong narcissistic functioning is indicative of what might happen, I would point to the emotional chasm they created between people, the pile of lies that eventually cannot be explained away, and the leaking that begins to happen among the narcissistic suppliers.

Narcissistic functioning requires constant reinforcement from others. Working with a megachurch, for example, I outlined the self-absorbed behavior of the lead pastor for the church board. "I don't care if he lies," a board member said, "because he brings so many people to Jesus." At the same meeting, the television evening newscaster for a local station defended the pastor, saying that everyone he knew who was successful in business was narcissistic.

The vice president of a dairy cooperative beamed when other employees mentioned that he turned a losing company into a winner. No one else could have done what he did. When people idealize a charismatic character, the flattery is inflated and scented with perfume. Some try to outdo others in the refueling process. The unreality of it all is appalling. You wonder if these people have brain injuries.

Narcissists themselves like to offer self-defense. "Steinke," an executive threatened me, "if you ruin things for me, I'll bury you." Offended by my report of his taking advantage of women employees, the owner of the company shouted at me, "What do you want me to do? Sit on my hands? When she dresses like that, it is an invitation. Forget my narcissism, or whatever you call it."

Lying is so natural; blaming is a daily exercise. Using others to do one's dirty work is common. Having seen one, you have seen the other fifteen. Sometimes I have marveled at how cunning and persuasive they can be, selling you hot chocolate in August on a day registering 80 percent humidity and 95 degrees, and you think you have iced tea. Then, too, you ask yourself, could anyone fall for this ruse? In the book *The People of the Lie*, psychiatrist Scott Peck noted that in the presence of the narcissist, you will get a sense of revulsion, a sense that this person is not normal, a caricature of being human.

THE LEADERSHIP NOTEBOOK

Reverse and Recognize

In part 1 below, I have listed characteristics of narcissistic functioning. An empty space is provided for noting the reverse behavior.

Part 1

1. I'm special. You are fortunate to have me as your leader. (Insert the opposite behavior here and below.)

2. I am unique and thereby entitled to have benefits.

3. Your admiration of me warrants a reward.

4. I live in the moment, instinctively.

5. If you offend me, I will skewer you.

6. If I say it is true, it is true.

7. I don't need counsel. I know best.

8. I don't take criticism well.

9. I never lose.

10. Expose me and you will pay for it.

Part 2

What can people do to detect a potential problem? When is the circle of charm most likely to form?

Questions to ask about another:

- Is this person too good to be true? Do we sense that something isn't right or missing when we talk to the person or observe his or her behavior?
- Have we carefully reviewed the person's history? What preceded this moment? What happened elsewhere?
- Why doesn't this person show any weaknesses or vulnerabilities? Why does this person always seem to be on top of the world? Did this person have disciples, groupies, or blind followers in past work situations?
- Does the person blame others, take the role of victim, or claim complete innocence of any past trouble?
- Is this person capable of self-awareness?

Questions for ourselves:

- Does our system have a good set of checks and balances? Can someone tilt the balance favorably in his or her direction without much effort? Is our system looking for a superstar, a mighty motivator, or a quick solution giver? Does our system think it is special?
- Do we use superlative words to describe what we want in a leader—dynamic, sharp, terrific, passionate, champion, charismatic?
- Are we looking for someone to relieve our depression or anxiety?
- Do we have an adequate feedback system? Can someone control information? Can people be propagandized?

THE LEADER'S CHALLENGE

Where there is the wind of change, some build walls; others build windmills.

—Chinese proverb

Differentiation cannot take place in a vacuum. It has to take place in relation to others.

—Murray Bowen

If your project does not have movement, then compared with the rest of the world, you're actually moving backward.

—Seth Godin

The (leader) has lost neutrality as completely when he or she is charmed as when angered.

—Daniel Papero

Our world is not becoming more stable or easier to comprehend. We are entering . . . a revolutionary age. And we are doing so with ideas, leaders, and institutions that are better suited for a world now several centuries behind us.

—Joshua Cooper Ramo

In a crisis, we tend to look for the wrong kind of leadership. We call for someone with answers, decision, strength, and a map of the future . . . who can make hard problems simple. . . . We should be calling for leadership that will challenge us to face problems for which there are no simple, painless solutions; problems that require us to learn new ways.

—Ronald A. Heifetz

10

ROCKING THE EMOTIONAL BOAT

SOMETHING HAS TO GIVE

Behind his desk, Colby Wells placed two framed quotes. Periodically, he would glance at them, but they were stored in his memory.

Frame 1: He who does not punish evil commands it to be done. (Leonardo da Vinci)

Frame 2: The evil of the wicked is proportionate to the weakness of the virtuous. (Winston Churchill)

Shortly after replacing Carlton Laird as the CEO of a small drug firm, he installed the frames. His predecessor had been complicit in the production of a skin cream that was based on falsified research. Some users of the product had irritated skin effects. It cost the company a stiff fine. The board forced Carlton to resign and placed Colby in the head position. Colby knew that the regulators, investors, and board members would be peering into his decision making with an eagle eye.

As a first step, Colby initiated a double testing; that is, all experimentation had to be tested twice by different testers before it could be considered for manufacturing. A few of the employees resisted, protesting the assumption that others would do what happened with the skin cream, "fudge" on the results. A group of chemists threatened to leave. Colby asked the protestors that if they intended to leave to give two weeks' notice. He didn't veer from his position; he saw the double test as a way to avoid what had happened and to ensure quality products. It had nothing to do with any individual's integrity. It protected everyone. The unhappy buzzing continued but dissipated with time. Colby Wells would be true to his word and wanted the same from others. Nonetheless, he was the target of rash comments and passive-aggressive behaviors. Colby had rocked the emotional boat.

RESISTANCE

The last people you expect to create a general disturbance are precisely the leaders of the system. However, a time comes when the leader may have to challenge individuals and the organization. A leader may have to upset the calm with distressing news, take action that will not prove popular, or make a decision that affects people's self-esteem and financial security. Such a time will require courage.

Emotional systems seek balance and stability. The technical term for this coherence is *homeostasis* (stay the same). In the human body, for instance, temperature, salt levels, and blood sugar levels are subject to homeostatic forces. When these levels drop or rise, the body automatically seeks to rebalance them. When leaders interrupt the system's balance, homeostatic forces push back—strangely, even if the alteration is positive or progressive. Someone becomes anxious in the unbalancing. No wonder I heard someone say, "Change is good; you go first."

The Indo-European word *leith*, for leader, means "to go forth, to die." In the Dutch vocabulary, one of the words for leader is translated "martyr"—one who suffers on behalf of another. It may not be foolish to ask, "How can I lead and not be wounded?" Capable, honest leaders have been depicted as inept and dishonest; the most effective leader may not be elected or selected from a gallery of candidates. Generally, people demand that leaders offer assurances and answers. Their expectation is that the leader will do this with a minimum of surprise or disruption.

Resistance is a natural component of the leadership process. Too many leaders are tempted to retreat or capitulate when resistance forms and becomes loud, rude, and messy. The unspoken rule may be "so as not to upset anyone." Leaders become pleasers, forsaking their birthright. Harvard professor of governance Ronald Heifetz states, "Followers want comfort, stability and solutions from their leaders, but that's babysitting. Real leaders ask hard questions and knock people out of their comfort zones. Then they manage the resulting distress." The "resulting distress" is what Bowen called emotional processes.

Humans have a strong tendency to group together. They find a sense of satisfaction in standing shoulder to shoulder and heart to heart. It is difficult for individuals who have a close bond to step back, look around, and see things objectively. Not wanting to be unpopular with the group, leaders may allow themselves to be co-opted by the group's emotional pressure.

The old Western myth of the hero-warrior—the lone, self-sufficient conqueror—is an old image, not really commensurate with the present emphasis on networking and participating with others. Still, it is a myth resurrected in times of Uproar, like the belief in a "final solution." Groups have always formed for protection, and when circumstances call for it, the group is ready for the redeemer, the white knight, or Superman/Superwoman.

In defense of the group, a research study put a monkey in a cage and exposed the animal to high levels of psychological stress, such as loud noises and flashing, bright lights. Nearly scared to death, the terrified monkey's stress hormone levels in its brain were measured. Next, the researchers introduced one change. They put another monkey in the cage, exposing both to the same loud noises and flashing lights. They took measure of the monkey's stress hormone level. It had dropped in half. The lone monkey was not good at handling stress, but the pair did well. Telling this story, I often ask, "Who's your monkey?" Obviously, we come together for fortification and support. The problem for the group is when it abdicates responsibility for its action and delegates it to a hero-warrior, when it looks outside itself for motivation.

ADAPTIVE PROBLEMS

It is commonplace for systems to deal with both technical and adaptive problems. The latter will surely set in place high anxiety with reactive behaviors. Technical problems are external and subject to know-how; adaptive challenges are hard to define completely, and no one knows for sure how to address them. They are issues for which there has to be an *internal* change, such as what one values or what one expects. Without the willingness of the leader to challenge people's ideas and behaviors, the leader will look for technical answers for adaptive issues. An excellent example of the technical/adaptive understanding of problems comes from medical history. Sherwin Nuland, clinical professor of surgery at Yale University, tells the incredible story of how medicine confused these two types of problems in the treatment of a long-standing illness. For thousands of years, women were dying of fever at childbirth. The prevailing opinion about its cause was so entrenched that new theories were ridiculed and easily dismissed. Here's the setting:

The physicians and nurses caring for the girl were all too familiar with the disease that took her young life. In 1847, one of every six mothers, like this young woman, was dying in the First Division of the Allgemeines Krankenhaus. The experience in this Vienna hospital was not unique; it was happening in hospitals throughout Europe. Childbed fever was rampant.

Twenty-two hundred years before, the disease had been described in the Hippocratic volume titled *Epidemics*. Even at that time, the cause of the disease was thought to be found in some stagnant or putrefied material whose source was within the body of the patient herself. An examiner of the disease, Dr. John Clarke (1793), referred to the disease as puerperal fever (*puer* = "child" and *parare* = "to bring forth"), believing that it was contagious, though this represented a minority viewpoint.

Oliver Wendell Holmes undertook a study of the problem of the transmission of the fever, thinking that it had infectious qualities and that physicians might be one of the carriers. But he was dismissed when an older doctor called his study "the meandering of a sophomore."

Puerperal fever continued to ravage the lives of young mothers because no one recognized the source—the hands of the physicians battling to prevent it. Doctors prior to delivery would examine cadavers, and because they did not sterilize their hands, they would bring foul particles from the lab into the clinic.

Ignac Semmelweiss started a new procedure, requiring medical students to wash their hands in a sanitizing solution before making an examination of the mother-to-be. The mortality rate declined. He published his results in a

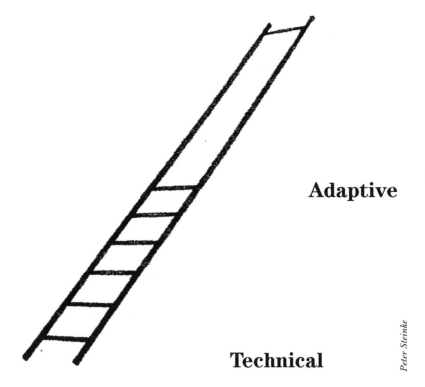

Adaptive

Technical

Peter Steinke

book that was rejected because his observation contradicted current medical beliefs, which blamed disease not on germs but on an imbalance of the "humors" in the body. Trivializing Semmelweiss's claims, the supervisor of the Allgemeines Krankenhaus attributed the improvement in statistics to a new ventilating system in the hospital. The situation required an adaptive response (integrating new learning) but received a technical one (the ventilating system). If Semmelweiss's theory had held in medical practice at that time, those who had believed otherwise would have experienced losses of credibility and authority.[1]

Some members of the nineteenth-century medical establishment had become so invested in their theory that new evidence could not be tolerated. "Adaptive change stimulates resistance," note Heifetz and Linsky, "because it challenges people's habits, beliefs, and values." The medical establishment's beliefs about the cause of the fever would have been jeopardized.

Systems will put up a struggle against taking new action but will also struggle against believing embarrassing news, upsetting messages, and shocking reports. When leaders upset the emotional system, they can't be surprised if people think their ideas are like "the meandering of a sophomore" or if people dismiss them by referring to their version of the Allgemeines Krankenhaus ventilating system. At highly anxious times, people regress. Their survival patterns are established, and very little is negotiable. Once the amygdala learns its lessons, learning stops. Employing primitive defense mechanisms, the agitated can see red but cannot see clearly. Though we may charge these resisters with being narrow-minded or parochial, they represent a human truth. No one likes to change, because loss of some type will occur. And loss will always bring along its cousin, disorientation.

THE ELEPHANT AND THE RIDER

I have placed the following information about the brain in this chapter because it is so pertinent to emotional functioning. We can better understand how natural it is to resist change and to ward off attempts at adaptive challenges. Neuroscientist Elkhonon Goldberg describes how our two brain hemispheres function in a different but complementary way. The right lobe is the place for receiving that which is novel, strange, and unfamiliar; the left lobe is about routine, the storage of known facts, and experiences. All new learning, therefore, begins on the right and proceeds to the left. One of the important questions that looms for the brain is, "Have I confronted this before?" If not, the right hemisphere of the brain, organized fundamentally to process novelty, will light up. On sight of a friend, the left hemisphere becomes active. Brain imaging will show a trained musician processing music in the left lobe and a novice activating the right lobe.

We learn by locating images, stories, and ideas in the left lobe that match the new situation in the right. We associate. Thus, the right lobe is always giving the left something to think about. When a match fails, we have to explore and imagine. But here is the catch-22. The right hemisphere is the location of the negative emotions of fear, disgust, and anger. When dealing with the new and unknown, it is easier to be apprehensive, distraught, or frustrated about it. On the left side, the positive emotions arise—joy and pleasure. Knowing something and being satisfied are easy companions. Familiarity does not so much breed contempt as it harbors a lot of knowns.

CHALLENGE

When new information comes through the right lobe, it may set off anger or fear if it contradicts the known lodged in the left lobe. If there is emotional interference, people may immediately or stridently deny the new data. Many times people go silent, another way to refute the distressing information. I have seen this silencing weave its way through a system. It's eerie.

When your left lobe (the archive of the known) has no image, replica, or similarity to what you hear or experience, doubt emerges. You, like all of us, want to search for, interpret, reinforce, and remember information that will confirm preexisting beliefs or assumptions—what is called *confirmation bias*. If your beliefs are deeply embedded and others oppose them, you will harbor strong, negative emotions. You are primed to find explanations that preserve your sense of reality. Everyone is biased toward information that supports their values or position. The confirmation could be a memory, an interpretation, a partisan position, an opinion, or a stereotype.

When you block out the new, the contrast, or the bizarre to preserve the known, you not only shrink your field of vision but also suffer "imaginative gridlock." You close the door to the left lobe; you lose the opportunity to associate the novelty you are experiencing with an array of other images or options. Unable to get past the emotional barriers of the right lobe, you're stuck. Wanting certainty, safety, and to be right, you reduce your attention to fresh ideas and emerging thoughts. Your anxiety shuts the door to the left lobe tightly.

Colby, having seen the deception of his predecessor, took the right lobe information (disturbing as it may have been) and released the lock on the left lobe, allowing the distress to come to left lobe attention. Others, though, were not ready to unlock their own left lobes, tied as they were to routine and habit.

Challenging people's preferences, questioning standard functioning, or proposing alternatives to routine activity, the leader will rattle people's right lobe, creating confusion that has been marinated in emotionality.

Neurologically, neurons that fire together wire together. Making new neuronal pathways is hard work. Disbelieving is wrenching. But with so much strangeness today, your right lobe can become calloused.

How much rocking the emotional boat can one tolerate? Colby did not count the cost or choose a non-confrontive approach. His wall hanging statements were classic reminders that silence can enable what is wrong or destructive, that fortification between the two lobes only produces getting dumber faster. Sheltering your confirmation biases is trafficking in convenience. Why rock the boat? Colby would answer: "Well, you will have to adapt to the changes. I was positioned here to oversee the system. For the well-being of all, a 'known' came to me that the weakness of the leader enables the deception of the system's practices. The boat will rock for a while. There has been deception. Together, we will restore the balance."

THE LEADER'S NOTEBOOK

Scanning the list of words below, mark the ones that would be the most difficult for you to face as a leader; then note which ones would be less demanding. Why the difference? Is the clue with the right or left lobe? Share your responses in a small group.

Item	Most Difficult	Less Difficult
Diversity		
Financial inequality		
Immigration		
Racial tension		
Religion		
Sexual harassment		
Social justice		
Gender issues		
Truth/fake news		
Betrayal		
Intimidation		
Lying/deception		
Physical threat		
Emotional blackmail		
Immature workers		
Upsetting the system		

11

WE VERSUS THEY

WEIRD NASTINESS

Nationally, the tenure for school superintendents is short-lived. At Elk Valley School District, three superintendents had served in the last nine years. The school board set two priorities for the incoming superintendent. They wanted to improve the graduation rate of high school students and slow the departure of many teachers.

When the board hired Constance Reed, they emphasized the two priorities. However, the teaching staff saw a different set of needs—raising the morale of the teachers (which also meant salary raises) and working on a plan to lower drug and alcohol use among the students. Teachers complained about student absences, sleeping in class, and incorrigible behavior. A "we versus they" arrangement was in place, mostly because the board operated in a top-down manner.

After a few months, Constance Reed saw the impasse and named it. She told the board that they would have to incorporate the two sets of expectations to avoid a clash. The board was quite stubborn and reminded Constance that her hiring depended on their priorities. She was caught in a triangle between the board and the teachers. We have learned that when anxiety "beefs up," interlocking triangles develop. Sure enough, school administrators brought their concerns, and different interest groups enlarged the playing field, each vying for attention and advantage. An anxious we and an anxious they set the stage for conflict.

With Uproar, conflict is a growth industry. Not only are the numbers of incidents rising, but also the number of people who can be stubborn, deceptive, and mean. Commenting about society in general, film critic Adam Gopnik claims that there is a growing "kind of weird, free-form nastiness—spleen without purpose." If conflict is intense and protracted, the battle drains the system's energy and resources.

"When you stir in conviction with anger," former educator Garret Keizer observes, "the anger is brighter, louder, and more willful. Add rage and the anger is wild." Meanwhile, some embroiled in the bitter rifts demand super-simple and immediate solutions—anything to ease their discomfort. Most people seek a quick return to normalcy. But the mere reduction of anxiety is fool's gold. The lessening of tensions is mistaken for resolution of the conflict. Restoration of equilibrium is not a sign that the system's functioning is improved. Certainly pain has receded. But leaders need to ask themselves, did the pain become a teacher? Did it provoke any new awareness? Did clarity develop to inform decision making? Were necessary changes implemented? If nothing is learned, if nothing changes, if important action is not taken, if new safeguards are not set in place, and if a sense of mission is not revived, the battle will return, maybe with different people over different issues, but not with different functioning. Essentially, the suffering will have yielded no benefit.

Conflict is a part of living. Often we react in a primitive way that results in a "we versus they" scenario. How we regard conflict is a test and an act of leadership. How can we turn trouble into opportunity? Most critically, when conflict arises, how can it be seen as a learning point for change and an experience that can strengthen the system's functioning? Not all conflicts are equal. Some are harsh and bitter. Yet many conflicts can contribute to the growth of a group and make a positive contribution. The quality of leadership applied to the situation significantly determines the outcome.

CONFLICT HABITS

For more than twenty-five years, I have consulted with more than two hundred systems engaged in conflict. I remind people that my intervention's purpose is that they do not waste their suffering. Conflict is a learning time, greatly depending upon the maturity and motivation of the system's leadership.

Bogged down in a standoff, people are apt to use conflict as a way of carrying out a competition, rather than as an education. The situation becomes increasingly negative and hostile. People are anxious about "losing" or appearing "weak" or being humiliated. This only stiffens their will to prevail.

Though not easily accomplished, what is required is action, not victory. Someone has to provide a way to focus and to engage the people's imaginative capacities. How can we move from argument to explanation? If we don't, we're entangled in nothing but a trial of strength. How can we use our ingenuity to address our predicament instead of defeating the other side? Leaders are needed who can help design an outcome instead of arbitrating or refereeing an emotional wrestling match.

We have learned ways to handle conflict that never lead to learning.

Neglect or Denial

Leaders may opt for denial to alleviate emotional discomfort, as if inattention could disable incredibly strong forces. Instead of giving in, leaders ignore. But a conflict suppressed only needs a new stroke of anxiety to excite reactivity once again. Anxiety deferred is not the same as anxiety managed.

Peace Mongering

Peace mongering is common. With tranquility and stability as premium values, leaders adapt to their most recalcitrant and immature people, allowing them to use threats and tantrums as levers of influence. Malcontents' complaints never seem to cease. Unwilling to confront the constant critic, leaders set the table for the unhappy souls to have a moveable feast of anxiety. By appeasing rather than opposing, leaders give control to reactive forces. Feed them once, and leaders can be sure they will be back for more.

False Attribution

Another habit is the attribution of blame. Blaming is a defensive behavior. It's an attempt to escape responsibility. Instead of saying, "I felt betrayed," we resort to, "Why did you turn against me?"

Quick Fix

When people have a low tolerance for pain, they are ready to accept snake oil remedies. Friedman stated, "People can rarely rise above the level of the maturity of their leaders or mentors. In every area of American civilization today, leaders and mentors are adapting to this demand for quick fixes . . . for problems that actually have to do with emotional processes."

IT'S THE EMOTIONAL PROCESS, DUMMY

Besides these conflict habits, systems are now experiencing an increase in belligerent behaviors. The following conflict scenario is repeated regularly: friction between two parties intensifies, a series of painful exchanges follows, the sides deadlock, and finally someone or some group requests or demands a person's removal or they threaten to remove themselves. Any removal would bring relief to some but fuel resentment among others. Instead of being conciliatory or engaging in problem solving, people become polarized. Group balance is disturbed more by people's strong reaction to one another than by reaction to the issue or the event itself. Polarization is emotionally maintained. The goal of conflict is to win. No thought is given to "we sink or swim together." Instead, one party swims and the other must sink. Bowen noted that when emotional tension intensifies, people split off into subsystems. "They become so emotionally embroiled with their differences," Bowen adds, "they can no longer see that they came from the same basic roots." They shift wanting to win toward wanting to hurt. Aggression is seldom physical; it is more often psychological, such as belittling and shaming the other party. Conflict is no longer a time for learning but for conquering. Domination supplants education. Civility and courtesy give way to sneers and shouting. Heat, not light, is the outcome. Author Garret Keizer notes, "One of the things we fear most is losing a battle. It is as if the primal emotion of anger arises in us because every conflict in some way recalls some primal conflict when our very lives were at stake."

When a conflict regresses to forceful competition, we are apt to see the following:

- People function at the level of the primitive brain, breaking everything into this or that, black or white, plus or minus. The primitive instinct neatly narrows complexity into "we versus they." In fact, some people gain support for their "side" by deepening the polarization, even promising to maintain it.
- Worse yet, when emotional juices are sprayed on the issues, fervor and passion knock reason out of the picture. The original differences themselves are no longer sustaining the differing. Emotionality drives the competition. When that happens, people will not respond to reasonableness, insight, or love. With yes-or-no thinking dividing the house, the objective all comes down to winning. Bring down the enemy!
- Behaviors become more aggressive—shouting down the opposite side, belittling them, using in-your-face tactics to intimidate, threatening legal action against someone, stacking the deck with supporters.

- Lying increases, taking many forms—half-truths, withholding information, inflating statistics and bloating claims, fabricating events, releasing publicly what was to be private, double-talk, false attributions, and claims of forgetfulness.
- Self-righteousness emerges. One party thinks she can use any means to achieve her end because her cause is "right." No one plays by the rules now. A person takes any advantage possible, even introducing God as ally.

> *Being right is not too difficult. You choose your perception; you select your information. You leave out what does not suit you, you drag in some general-purpose value words, you throw in a sneer or two about the opposition, and you are a fine fellow who has made a fine speech.*
>
> —Edward de Bono[1]

ROGUE CELLS

While viruses are foreign substances that invade and manipulate the body's cells for their own purposes, cancer is a disease with its own destructive pattern. A collection of cells that function in ways distinct from normal cells, cancer cells function like "disease" in human relationships:

- Unlike normal cells, cancer cells recklessly overproduce. Cancer cells grow. And multiply. Grow and multiply. This is the reason cancer specialists refer to these cells as "immortal" (at least until they kill the cells of which they are a part). Normal cells have a programmed cell death, called apoptosis, that allows the cells to die and make room for new cells. Cancer cells follow no such commands. They live for themselves.
- Cancer cells lack the mechanism to stick together. They break away to attach themselves to surrounding cells (this process is called metastasis). The normal cohesion between cells can be weakened, and malignant cells separate from the original mass and travel elsewhere.

- Normal cells eventually differentiate, becoming part of bone and muscle. Cancer cells, however, "dedifferentiate." Somehow along the way, tumor cells lose their capacity to differentiate. Malignant cells do not become part of the mission of the living tissue. They say to the rest of the organism, "We have no need of you. We are the center of the universe. Your job is to feed us." As with so many immature individuals, what they do is uncoordinated with the needs or constraints of their neighbors. Having no regard for the rest of the body, these disloyal cells live for themselves, pursuing their own interests in conflict with the host.

Dealing with people who function in a me-only manner is time consuming and energy draining. They are determined to have it their way, regardless.

Leaders must provide an immune response. But what happens when the leadership itself is divided? One group will see the functioning of a "foreign substance" or "intruder" and another group a "normal" cell. The stalemate can lead to a healthy struggle around such questions as:

How are we going to function as a community?
What is our defining and unique mission?
What are the norms to which we hold each other accountable?
What are the expectations of each member with regard to the whole?

Contrariwise, the leadership's division puts the immune response on hold.

PAY ATTENTION

For you, the leader, there are no off-seasons, because every season under the sun requires leadership. All seasons are important, but none more so than the strong season when emotions run high. Uproar begs for attention. I have found these responses to be beneficial:

1. *Respecting the sheer strength of survival instincts.* The will to survive is extremely strong. Brains are constructed, at first, to react to threat,

not contemplate it. In the presence of high tension, expect behavior to be substandard for a while. Being patient in order to move toward improvement, the leader will not make choices driven by the anxiety of the moment. Thoughtfulness will reappear as primitive instincts subside. First, however, the craziness has to play itself out: blaming, misinforming, taking defensive action, shouting impassioned comments, repeating unfounded rumors, exaggerating events, and relying on worst-case consequences.

2. *Seeking clarity.* With misinformation, rumor, and exaggeration bouncing off the wall, confusion is always in attendance. Ask questions. Weigh whether information is reliable and congruent. But also remember that clarity won't always be comfortable for everyone. Some people will wear emotional blinders. Stay on course. Ultimately, people prefer hearing the truth rather than distortion.

3. *Observing behavior.* Bowen theory is a promising advancement in both understanding systems conflict and regulating its noxious effects. The theory describes the human family as a natural, living, multigenerational system in which each person's functioning affects all the other members' functioning. Bowen contended that human systems function in ways similar to other life forms. What distinguishes the human family from the rest of nature is the human capacity to observe automatic behavior and substitute principles for impulses, developing more thoughtful approaches to life's challenges.

As I discussed in chapter 1, Bowen used the terms *emotional* and *emotionality* to signify behavior that is impulsive and instinctual. Remember the lizard. Emotionality is wired into our protoplasm for rapid, defensive purposes and is necessary for us to confront threats and to survive. Emotional processes are driven by automatic behaviors. Sometimes, instead of acting rationally, we flare up in anger or pull back in fear. At other times, we maintain our composure and retain our ability to think things through.

Imagine a person in your system who is a habitual complainer. No matter what the condition, issue, or topic, the person will find something wrong. But the complainer is only half of the equation. In order for the carping censure to continue, others must reinforce it. Sometimes this happens by adding fuel to the fire, counterattacking the attacker. One way to be a non-anxious presence is not to be present. Sometimes the behavior is maintained because others cut themselves off from the critic. But distancing merely raises the stakes for the unhappy soul, and the complaints become deeper or more frequent. For any conflict to continue and get out of control, a generator of anxiety and an amplifier are needed. They feed each other.

4. *Informing.* In the early stages of a conflict, it is almost impossible to overinform. As much information as possible is needed. Providing information tends to minimize the need for people to create information for themselves through gossip and embellishments of what they have heard. By communicating forthrightly, leaders also treat the members as mature adults who can handle whatever information is shared, not as children who need to be protected from bad news.

5. *Working with the healthy individuals.* To move beyond people's survival instincts, leaders will be more successful when they work with the most mature, motivated people in the system. No one can pour insight into unmotivated people. The unmotivated individual may be on both sides of the conflict.

6. *Structuring a process.* An anxiety-infected system spreads anxiety in all directions. People increasingly become confused, angry, and disgusted and inch toward near despair. The flow of anxiety needs to be contained, and nothing does this better than placing a structure over the anxiety-ridden field. When people sense that there will be an orderly effort in place, they think things are not totally out of control. People yearn for clear and decisive action. When specific goals are followed, the people have confidence that the system has the means to get out of the misery they have gotten into and to move forward again. Good structure corrals anxiety.

7. *Reframing the situation.* Instead of anxiously bemoaning what's happening, leaders can frame the situation as an opportunity for growth. Through this painful encounter, the system will emerge stronger, knowing better ways to live together.

8. *Building up the system's positive emotional bank account.* Once a conflict subsides, leaders provide aftercare, which could embrace many options. John Gottman, a marriage researcher, believed that marriage counselors spent too much time helping couples to fight fair or to learn

how to handle their partner better. Gottman suggested that counselors should spend more time helping marriage partners promote a steady flow of positive interactions in their relationship, which, according to longitudinal studies, is a critical ingredient of long and rewarding marriages. Building up a robust emotional bank account of goodwill, fun, care, and respect serves marriage more than reducing fighting does. Moreover, the account draws interest. Dr. Friedman called it focusing on strength, not pathology. Systems benefit from their steady flow of positive programs and supportive gatherings. When tensions threaten relationships, people can draw from their positive emotional investments as a resource to move past the pressing moment. People know that the system, even if in tension, is a safe place.

9. *Bringing in a third party.* Some conflict becomes so convoluted and emotional that those affected become entrenched in their "our side" bias. The parties involved in a dispute are too closely involved to get a wider view. To dislodge the ensuing impasse, an outside third party with a more objective set of eyes is needed. Select someone outside of the emotional system who will be fair and frank. The people involved in the dispute are too close to what is happening to get an overview or to get a sense of perspective. It is also difficult for them to carry out the thinking operations necessary to bring clarity to a situation when emotional factors run strong. With strong emotionality, people construct an argument to support their viewpoint rather than explore other points of view.

THE LEADER'S NOTEBOOK

Twenty Observations

I have worked with troubled systems for more than twenty-five years. I continue to learn from these experiences. The list below includes some of what I have learned about systems in times of conflict.

1. Most people are more interested in relieving their anxiety than in managing the crisis or planning a clear direction. Their primary goal is anxiety reduction, not renewal.
2. Under certain conditions, anxiety is neutral. As much as possible, effective leaders normalize anxiety. Considering what is happening, anxiety's presence is what you would expect. By normalizing, people will not automatically think the community is flawed.
3. If anxiety is high, people lose their capacity to be self-reflective. They look outward, not at themselves. Self-awareness is dim. And the ability to identify with the life processes of others is impaired.
4. Peace is often preferred over justice. People can resist or be hesitant about taking stands, making decisions, or charting a course of action that would offend or upset the community. By placing a premium on togetherness, they play into the hands of the most dependent people, who can threaten to incite disharmony as a way of receiving what they want. When superficial harmony prevails, the pursuit of justice is sacrificed.
5. If an individual becomes the lightning rod for people's anxiety and cannot extricate him- or herself from that position through self-differentiation (or the environment is so perverse that no one can escape from that position), trying to maintain one's position or presence in the emotional system is unproductive as well as painful.
6. All disease processes are enabled. Viruses need host cells. Not all people designated by anxious systems as the patient are sick. The illness is in the interactive system, to which the following observations attest:

All neuroses have accomplices (Carl Jung).

Anxiety not resolved in one relationship will be acted out in another relationship.

Unless the leader has a degree of self-knowledge and self-understanding, there is the risk that he or she may use the organization to address his or her own neuroses (Peter Senge et al.).

7. The way we use information is an emotional phenomenon; what we hear and don't hear, what we remember, and how we gather and exclude data are all connected to emotional processes. We gravitate toward information that coincides with our viewpoints and that promises to contribute to our survival.

8. The healing process for midrange to severely anxious systems takes time.

9. Losses will result, no matter what choices are made.

10. Secrets—that is, hidden agendas and invisible loyalties—in most cases need to be brought to light.

11. Reactivity can issue from people who are leaders, erudite, talented, wealthy, well educated, pious, charming, or normally calm folks. None of the above characteristics indicate that these individuals are emotionally mature.

12. Issues must be clearly identified, and individuals must be challenged to act. No anxious system can handle more than three to five issues at a time. The issues must be condensed.

13. Sabotage of the process for dealing with conflict should be expected. The usual saboteurs will be those who are losing control or not getting what they want from it.

14. Murray Bowen claimed that all dyads are unstable. Therefore, the basic molecule of all relationship systems is a triangle (the use of a third party to reduce tension between a twosome). A Swahili proverb reads, "When the elephants fight, it's the grass that gets crushed." Triangle formation is natural. Triangling is another matter. It happens when the third party allows the original dyad to escape responsibility for its actions by assuming their anxiety and taking responsibility for them. Whenever a system brings in a third party, such as an intervention team, there is a triangle.

15. Five styles of managing conflict have become commonplace: accommodating, problem solving, compromising, avoiding, and fighting. They are useful for recognizing general patterns of behavior under pressure. But they are not helpful when used as predictors—"Oh, Susan never takes a stand. She'll compromise on anything." People like Susan do not function in the same way in every context. At home, Susan may compromise; but at work, she's quite a problem solver. Pseudo-selves are willing to trade off functioning positions.

16. Recent research challenges the prevailing assumptions about conflict behavior. For example, direct fighting and problem solving are more effective in combination than they are in isolation.

17. People become more involved if they anticipate losses as a result of the conflict than if they anticipate gains. Losses arouse greater emotional force.

18. No emotional system will change unless the members of the system change how they interact with one another. Patterns of behavior tend toward rigidity. Conflict may be necessary to jolt and jar the shape of things in order to reshape the pattern.

19. The parties involved in a rift are in a poor position to settle the dispute if anxiety is high and rampant. Being too closely and emotionally involved in a circumstance, they will find it difficult to provide a fair overview or a genuine perspective.

20. Final or perfect solutions are not available. Conflict leaves things messy. The best solutions to insolvable problems are the approximate solutions—ones that prepare a system for new learning and a new beginning.

12

STAYING CALM AND COURAGEOUS, NO MATTER WHAT

ENDURANCE

Tamara Chan, a petite woman with a ready smile and a gentle voice, attended a workshop I led titled "Leadership in an Emotional System." At the time, she was the vice president of a garden club. Several years later, she emailed me after she had been elected a state representative. Being in state government, she came to the position with energy and enthusiasm. But after she had a rude verbal collision with a senior member of the assembly, she needed to talk to someone. A veteran lawmaker urged her to be "quiet" and to learn the ropes as a political yearling. As a penalty for taking public stands, she was assigned to a low-level committee. Having been an official in a garden club, you can imagine that she had keen interest in environmental affairs. With impending legislation regarding the environment at hand, she spoke against relaxing the rules concerning the disposal of industrial waste and for clean water. She also joined hands with a group that wanted new rules for reforestation. To her, it was obvious that many of her colleagues were either uninformed or misinformed about the real issues.

We arranged a time for a telephone conversation. She noted that there were some earnest, solid individuals who wanted to protect the environment. But the downside of serving in the chamber was those who were too rigid or flaccid in their views of the environment. One legislator brutally told her,

"Women are to be seen." A second person warned her that she was agitating the moderator, who thought she was lecturing him. Saddened, she felt that no one was willing to consider alternatives to their preferred views, fastened as they were to their prejudices, stereotypes, or patronage. "I'm feeling the pressure to back off," she said, "and be a child again." She compared it to the times her parents would tell her to go to her room and clean it. In an ideal forum designed for discovery, she had to tolerate demeaning comments and put aside her disturbing questions.

I gave her feedback: she sounded as anxiously helpful as others were anxiously adamant. Could she be more playful? I said she was responsible for the position of leadership, not the champion of good causes. And mature leadership meant you had to stay the course and allow time for things to process.

She acknowledged that Bowen's concept of differentiation was not a simple task. On the one hand, she did not want to capitulate to the conformists, and neither did she want to distance herself from them. A couple of years ago, Tamara sent me a Christmas card in which she enclosed a picture of herself holding two jars of water. In her left hand was a jar with sediment and in the other hand a jar of clean water. Below the picture, she wrote,

> As Dr. Friedman said, you have to take a punch, persevere, and stay the course. Didn't Shackleton enter the dangerous Antarctic with a ship dubbed *Endurance*? If you are anxious, you lose patience and ground—and think the resisters are the problem.

SURVIVAL OR CHALLENGE

Leadership is an extraordinary opportunity to address the needs of people and direct their energies toward a common purpose. You draw people's attention to something larger than themselves. In highly anxious times, people become more demanding, however, about meeting their needs, and leaders are tested in new ways. The common purpose you share becomes diffused. The larger view is lost in the pressure of the moment.

Even beyond these anxious periods, a leader has to contend with normal stresses. The notion that authority cannot be trusted is prevalent today. Leaders are regularly criticized. People in any organization settle into a comfort zone and refuse to budge. People's expectations of you reach unrealistic proportions—keep everyone's spirit high, discourage any negative talk, stay loyal to the community's values, eliminate vexing questions, maintain calm for the sake of togetherness. Sometimes the expectation is, "Remember, you are not authorized to push us, quiz us, or surprise us. If you want to be liked, don't get ahead of us. Be our leader, but keep following us." The leader is effectively neutralized.

Leadership brings you assaults and roadblocks. Yet leadership doesn't mean that you have to sacrifice yourself or be sacrificed by someone else. Leadership has many other possibilities. No doubt, periods of stress bring on automatic survival needs. Instincts take over. The protective part of the brain is in control. Once the environment feels safe again, a new imperative—to stretch and push forward—may emerge. *No choice is more important than whether you choose to be a leader who gets bogged down in survival or one who rises to the level of challenge.* Are you driven by the impulsive reactions of others or your own survival instincts? Do you serve thoughtfully and courageously?

Since nature has prepared us to be afraid of real or imagined threats, we are innately designed to avoid danger. We turn to our survival instincts. The amygdala incites anxious reactions. Once our primitive survival brain rules, we are driven to reflexive behaviors. At the same time, our reflective capacities are constricted, limiting the range of responses we might make. All the advantages a left prefrontal cortex provides—hindsight, insight, and foresight—seem to be lost at once.

Only when automatic processes are interrupted in some way are the automatic outcomes changed. Only when we see the crisis before us as not simply a matter of survival but also a matter of challenge is adaptive change possible. But adaptive change requires a period of disorientation—"a formless void and darkness." We don't know what is coming next. We find ourselves in a strange wilderness. The safe, known world with all of its pleasurable feelings is gone for a time, and not until we live out that time can we come to a reorientation.

UNDER PRESSURE

Under great pressure, systems destabilize, and people stagger in no-man's-land. Leaders are faced with three fundamental patterns: (1) the quick fix, (2) wait and see, and (3) adaptive practice.

Pattern One—Quick Fix

A series of unfavorable events occurs, or a slow stream of negative happenings are unattended to and anxiety rises, shattering the harmony and coherence in the system. People's behaviors are quite predictable, such as maximizing the seriousness of the problem, resorting to irrational arguments, lots of fault finding, and a painful anxiety that drives toward a final solution. ASAP signals are everywhere.

A leader acts to placate or rescue those who are emotionally threatened or incensed. They do not get outside of the anxious system to take thoughtful stands. Rather, they offer immediate comfort to quell the storm. There is no learning.

Reacting to Tamara Chan, several assemblymen applied the quick fix to keep her quiet, reminding her of her rookie status, her role to be seen and not heard, and her disrupting demeanor. To reduce their own anxiety, they wanted to silence her quickly.

Pattern Two—Wait and See

This pattern is less trigger-like but still subject to emotional forces. A preliminary period is set aside for the fog to lift and the noise to abate. The leader knows the emotional clamor needs to be tempered before thoughtful action can be taken. Wait and see, however, can be used as a delay tactic in the hope that anxiety will subside or wilt. Yet it would take only a few anxious souls to create a rerun of the disturbance. Like a traffic signal, the yellow caution light yields to either red or green for a decision. Putting anything on hold or kicking the can down the road offers time but not a solution.

After the killing of seventeen people in Parkland, Florida, the leader of the House of Representatives, Paul Ryan, said for the fifth consecutive time following one of these shootings that we needed to wait before jumping to conclusions. Senator Marco Rubio weakly suggested that this was not a time to discuss gun control. Both are anxious, diversionary moves.

Pattern Three—Adaptive Practice

Life is a process of reacting (reactors) and responding (actors). We react because we have survival needs; we respond because we have challenge needs. To meet challenge needs, no responses are more important than staying calm and being courageous, *no matter what*. When calm, a leader can access clear thinking, and when courageous one can act on principles. Both are advantages, since the leader will have a greater repertoire of responses to deal with circumstances. One is always limited by instinctive behavior, the preprogrammed, automatic behaviors of fight, flight, or freeze.

You will recall Shackleton's portrayal of calmness and courage in the face of horrible odds. Trapped in the vise of Antarctic ice, Shackleton began to talk to his crewmates about a future exploration in the northern Arctic. Musing about the burden of responsibility, he acknowledged being lifted up by the men's good cheer. Shackleton and his crew were in an oscillating story of deadly seriousness and surprising joviality. The days of desperation were counterbalanced by a spontaneous celebration that included libation, story-telling, and good banter. Even more, having chosen the right tone—"calm, confident, and reassuring"—Shackleton's presence kept his crew from succumbing to the protracted strain. In his diary, Captain Worsley noted how Shackleton's "putting on a good face" or merely being there stimulated a pervasive spirit of hope. We don't know much about Shackleton's family, but the family's Latin motto tells about the values with which he lived: *Fortitudine vincimus* (By endurance, we conquer). Psychological hazards are part of any exploration, and the leader's composure and poise can be as much a factor in shaping outcomes as anxiety.

THE STORIED LIFE

Studying the American family, psychologist Marshall Duke claimed, "We were blown away!" Duke and several assistant researchers discovered that children who knew a lot about their family's history did better later in life when they themselves were challenged.[1] Knowing the ups and downs of their families prepared them to be more resilient and proactive, moderating the effect of stress. They were able to influence the outcomes in their lives, avoiding any semblance of what Bowen called "functional helplessness."

When the researchers accumulated hundreds of stories, they discovered that the themes coincided with Christopher Booker's notation in his book *The Seven Basic Plots: Why We Tell Stories*. Duke mentioned that the choice of what story to tell revealed the values of the narrator. In addition, he associated the process of storytelling with other processes that help children develop well, such as openness to excruciating dilemmas (no secrets) and awareness of failure (not the end of the story).

As the children in the study matured, the researchers found that the children had higher levels of self-esteem, more inner locus of control, greater belief in their capacity to accomplish things, lower levels of anxiety, and better family functioning. Storytelling enhanced the self as an agent, a responsible/responsive being.

From the moment there is an exchange between brain and context, our interactions begin to form a template, shape neural pathways, and switch on genes. Over time, the repeated pattern of dealing with experiences—whether anxiety, conflict, disapproval, support, encouragement, or security—starts to define who we are. All of this happens with a nervous system biased toward survival and social response. Ideally, the interchange between physiology and environment leads to a responsibly functioning human being. When, however, the interchange has been non-productive, alienating, or apathetic, it degenerates into anxiety and insecurity. Nurture fails nature.

Our families have stories. We are products of our familial context, from generation to generation. No less than Carl Jung, a disciple of Freud, understood that when we do family-of-origin work (discovering the narrative that preceded us), we take the leftovers from the past so that we can be better equipped to create for ourselves the kind of life we want. We build on past plots. The purpose is to change self, to author the next chapter.

Our identities are wrapped up with those who came before us and among whom we live. "I am what I am," an African sage noted, "because of who we all are." Further, no two families are alike, which makes each person special. "It's a fingerprint" (Marshall Duke). The context of the story lives on, or as someone said, "the presence of the past" goes with us. We are all part of what came before. Psychologist William James boldly stated, "An impression can be so exciting emotionally to leave a scar upon cerebral tissue."

BOWEN'S SURPRISE

Murray Bowen, too, recognized yesterday's presence in today's functioning. He developed the family diagram (often called the genogram) to outline the family's plots over three to four generations. The genogram depicted birth order, interactions between family members, emotional fusion or cutoff, different roles members of the family play, the family projection process, and other facets of the emotional system.

Bowen knew that the "self" is a product of the family relationship system. A well-developed self emerges from the family, if one is not too invested in the family's emotional system. One can differentiate at a higher level if one is not stuck reacting to the family. It is at this point that some find Bowen's thinking problematical. Why the strong emphasis on "self"? What about others? Isn't this antithetical to what was said in the chapter "The People of the Charm"? We assume that a focus on self will lead to self-absorption, arrogance, egotism, and indifference toward others. Bowen contended the opposite. A focus on self will automatically place a focus on others. To value self, to believe in one's abilities, and to be responsible for one's own functioning carries over in response to others. He sounds counterintuitive, saying that a person working toward responsibility in self is always aware of one's responsibility to other people. Giving energy to being responsible, one becomes more responsive to others, and at the same time less irresponsibly overinvolved with others. Focusing on one's own functioning naturally leads to permitting others as much latitude as possible toward developing their own selves. Some have seen this as Bowen's way of reaffirming the ethic of loving others as you love yourself.

As to leadership, think of what this means. If you are irresponsibly overinvolved in the lives of others, you may protect ineffective staff members. If you have strong rescue needs, you will spend an inordinate amount of time and effort to fix things. You will lose a sense of objectivity. You will listen to the loudest voices too often.

If one is focused on one's own functioning, how does this differ from narcissistic functioning? First, you need to remember that narcissistic functioning is automatic behavior. It's like sneezing. Second, the person exhibiting this behavior needs the constant fueling of one's grandiosity from outside sources. There's a dependency on others. But becoming a responsible/responsive self is intentional work. It does not require the flattery or projection of greatness from others. Caring for self and caring for others flow in one stream, separately. Narcissism is emotional fusion between two needy selves. Two manipulative selves (the charmer and the charmed) do not make a responsible relationship. Each is irresponsibly overinvolved with the other. The narcissist cannot give as much latitude as is possible for the other to grow. If the other grows, the fuel needed might not continue.

THE LIVING PAST

How, you wonder, does this relate to leadership? Family therapist Monica McGoldrick claims that there is a relationship between knowing more about our families and knowing more about ourselves. As a result, we have the awareness and freedom to determine how we want to live. Through self-discovery, we can become more responsible selves, aware of our automatic tendencies and our patterns of functioning. The family diagram can be an instrument for change. In *Composing a Life*, the author Mary Catherine Bateson asserts that designing a life will be a combination of "reimagining of the future and reinterpreting of the past." The word *freedom* is significant since it points to the choices and options we have in the present, free to move beyond the patterns we have learned in the family. Bowen therapists encourage leaders to do family-of-origin work in order to function in more intentional ways.

Having heard about Duke's research at a storytelling workshop, Maria Mendez applied it to her classroom. She asked her students to complete Duke's "Did You Know" questions. If they did not know the answers, they were to ask their parents and relatives. The students exchanged stories from their family's past. At another time, she asked the students to tell stories that they would like to share with their children or grandchildren in the future (something from their own experience). During the course of the year, she asked the students to focus on one of several questions she had written down, such as what their birth order position is like in their family; if they moved to another location and had to attend a new school, what did it feel like; who in the extended family did they most admire or respect, and similar questions—and to tell the story orally.

She was not sure how to measure the results. Was anxiety lowered? Were there fewer behavior problems? Were there higher grades? At the end of the school year, she asked her class what the most beneficial learning experience was. Twenty-three of twenty-eight students cited the DYK exercises. Twelve-year-old Sonya shared how she learned to deal with her eight-year-old brother. She said any girl in the class that had a younger brother had become a "feminist." Her brother Farley pestered her continually. He did things to irritate her in order to get her attention. She would hit him or shout loudly in reaction. But she remembered a story her grandmother told her about how one of her bosses would always complain to her grandmother. Every month her grandmother gave her boss a pad and asked him to write down the complaints and give it to her at the end of the week. Soon, he stopped pestering her. Reactivity generated requires reactivity amplified. Emotionality rules this pattern of behavior.

Daniel Hart and Abdul Gjante became friends in college and started a small business—Maid for You. It was a residential cleaning service originally but eventually included industrial sites. Daniel read Bruce Feiler's article in the *New York Times* titled "The Family Stories That Bind Us" (March 2013). He wondered if the same results might happen if applied to a business (another emotional system). He and Abdul inserted into their training program a time for storytelling, including how they met, dreamed up a business, put it together, worked through troubling times, and what they learned. The new trainees were given more than mops and buckets, but also a glimpse of history and the freedom to share their stories.

Again, the two of them, like Maria, were not sure how to evaluate the DYK and history sharing. They were surprised to hear when preparing for another training program that those who had attended last year's training wanted something like the previous year's. Sheila and Tate revealed they had become closer and enjoyed working with one another, knowing each one's story. Pablo took the storytelling venture home and found that it helped his family's functioning.

In Feiler's article, he noted that, at the Naval Academy, a commander advised graduating seniors to take incoming freshmen or plebes on history-building events, such as visiting a cemetery to pay tribute to the first naval aviator's burial ground and visiting a historical display of aviation.

In any group, about 40 percent will be mostly visual learners (videos, diagrams, pictures), and another 40 percent will be auditory learners (lectures, discussion, sound). The remaining 20 percent are kinesthetic learners (doing, performing, experiencing). Storytelling has aspects of all three ways of learning. Further, storytelling is a way of activating both the thinking and feeling brains simultaneously. Knowing and sensing come together.

"Every great leader," Howard Gardner said, "is a great storyteller." Another sage remarked that the six most powerful words in any language are "Let me tell you a story." When we sleep and dream, we are inventing new tales. When we attend the movies, a concert, or an art museum, we are immersed in a narrative. I recently visited the Museum of Modern Art in New York City and spent an hour looking at and reading about Louise Bourgoise. The spiders, the painted cloth, and the sculptures came alive as I learned of her family's history, especially the emotional pain. Perhaps we have missed the incredible potential there is in sharing and telling stories for the effectiveness of leadership. Is this not a source for calmness and courage, knowing the oscillating nature of life?

THE LEADER'S NOTEBOOK

Marshall Duke's DYK chart asked such questions as those below.[2] If you were to assemble a similar chart for your system, what questions would you ask? Ten spaces are provided, with a couple of initial suggestions.

1. Do you know how your parents met?
2. Do you know some of the jobs that your parents had when they were young?
3.
4.
5.
6.
7.
8.
9.
10.

POSTSCRIPT

B owen theory describes differentiation of self as a process whereby a person proceeds toward a more *thoughtful* and *responsible* position in life. It is a lifelong process requiring years of learning and practice aided by a high level of motivation and doses of courage.

The differentiation pattern is a unique expression of leadership. It doesn't look like the familiar form or general approach that we associate with a lead person. The differentiated leader acts on principle, stays connected with others, has an interest in their ideas (even if the people are known to be "difficult"), regulates his or her own anxiety, and follows a self-chosen direction. This is not the usual leader in American society. The mature leader does not blame others, does not instruct them on what to do, does not claim godlike powers, does not pursue "peace at any price," but does accept a part in any problem or situation where appropriate, does less reacting to the reactivity of others, does work toward proximate solutions to insolvable problems, and does avoid imposing emotional pressure on others to achieve conformity. The key realization is that one's own thoughtful and responsible functioning goes a long way toward resolving and repairing systemic issues. A differentiated leader is not like the charismatic individual who sets off fireworks and lights up the sky. Leadership is about maturity, not wizardry.

BEST THINKING

> *The most important difference between man and lower forms is his cerebral cortex and his ability to think and reason. Intellectual functioning is regarded as distinctively different from emotional functioning, which man shares with the lower forms.*

—Murray Bowen[1]

Dr. Bowen would have us do our best *thinking*, which is our unequalled human distinction. We can overcome the dictates of our biological heritage; we do not have to react automatically to the world. Unlike other creatures, human beings have expanded mental capacities. With no two neurons alike and each neuron connected to thousands of others, issuing and receiving signals to one another, crossing a myriad of relay stations known as synapses, operating with chemistry and electricity, eighty-six billion neurons make us capable of paying attention, observing, being conscious, making choices, creating designs, comparing elements, changing our minds, figuring out complex formulas, and using symbols for comprehension. Having language as our guide, we give meaning/purpose to our lived experience, envision possibility, enjoy relationships, and consider the future. With the inheritance of language, the thinking brain has a "head start," as long as the lower brain does not get there first.

Sometimes we overplay the mental side (intent) to the detriment of the emotional side (instant). "Whoever said, I think, therefore I am," Milan Kundera states, "had to be someone who underrated toothaches." Bowen never pitted cognition and emotion against each other. Instead, he wanted to affirm that both are processes of information with different functions. The emotional forces work best in emergencies, and thought serves best when understanding and planning are needed.

Variously termed "the crowded chemistry lab," "the enchanted loom," "the three-pound universe," "the vault of heaven," and "the huddle of neurons calling all the plays," the brain still draws questions about its effectiveness. No less than Charles Darwin pushed the envelope of caution:

With me, the torrid doubt always arises whether the convictions of men's mind, which has been developed from the mind of the slower animal, are of any value or at all valuable.

Could our deep pondering have no significance since our minds are derivatives of lesser beings?

Going further, Georg Christoph Lichtenberg wondered if it is possible to tell the difference between what is sane and what is crazy: "We cannot know whether we are not at the moment in a madhouse." Biologist Theodore Dobzhansky says we like to believe that if we offer adequate data bearing on scientific problems, "then anybody with normal intelligence will necessarily arrive at the same conclusion demonstrated, settled, proved, and established," yet no evidence is strong enough to have acceptance of a conclusion that is emotionally distasteful. Emotional interference can block the best of proof. Climate change? Russian interference? Police shootings? Fake news? Guns and mass murders?

When Newton proposed the existence of universal gravity, his contemporaries charged him with selling out to the mystics. Emotionally perturbed, they disparaged Newton. If you don't like the message, shoot the messenger (as a side note, Winston Churchill said that nothing is more exhilarating in life than to be shot at and missed).

A British surgeon discovered the medicinal value of lemons and limes in the treatment of scurvy. Given scarce credence, the facile rejection led to the needless deaths of British soldiers.

A limitation of the mind is revealed in the report of Darwin's expedition to Tierra del Fuego. The natives were fascinated with the small boats, which were comparable to their own. Yet they were oblivious to the larger vessel anchored off-coast. They had no counterpart in their own experience, no way to associate the anchored craft with something in their left lobe library. The right lobe didn't even bother the left lobe with the data of the large ship.

Despite defaults and limitations, the brain impacts all aspects of our lives. More now than ever before, we better do our best thinking. Uproar unsettles our nerves (anxiety), disturbs our worldview (our ideation may fail us and we could collapse into chaos), and turns reality into a guessing game (fake news). We react to it all. The lower brain is there for survival, has been around a lot longer than the thinking brain, is quicker, and knows how to keep anxiety happy. This brain knows its strength, even if it knows nothing else.

MOST RESPONSIBLE

> *The differentiation of self has to do with the levels of solid self and pseudo-self in a person. . . . The solid self says, "This is who I am, what I believe, what I stand for, and what I will do and will not do." . . . The pseudo-self is created by emotional pressure . . . the level of solid self is lower and the pseudo-self is much higher in all of us than most are aware. . . . Pseudo-self is an automatic emotional process.*
>
> —Murray Bowen[2]

Bowen would have us function in the most *responsible* way (with self-awareness, intentionality, and principled choices). He used the concepts of the solid self and the pseudo-self to distinguish two ways of living. The solid self is not negotiable; it is based on values, convictions, and beliefs. Commonly, we call this person genuine or authentic. One's integrity is not for sale. Opposite this position, Bowen says, is the pseudo-self, which is negotiable. This is the person that puts self up for auction. There is always a contract conditioning behavior. Principles may be espoused, but they are relaxed or ignored.

A vivid illustration of the two different ways of functioning is the biblical story of two brothers, Moses and Aaron. Moses leads the people of Israel out of Egypt (known as the Exodus), where they have been the despairing minions of Pharaoh. Released from his heavy rule, they make a trek through the wilderness, a rocky, grim terrain. Now, though, the oppression comes from hunger, thirst, and exhaustion. The food is monotonous, the nights are cold, and the days are uneventful.

Dissatisfied, the people complain against Moses and suggest that he has led them into this desolate landscape to die. Being in a sour mood, they lament having left Egypt. With a shortened memory, they recall the melons, cucumbers, and lemons they enjoyed there, forgetting the backbreaking work of making bricks. The writer of the book of Exodus states the situation succinctly: "They would not listen to Moses because of their broken spirit." With tempers flaring and reason disappearing, the people are ready to stone. Uproar!

MOSES

Two Types of Self

The next thing we know is Moses has left the tribe in search of spiritual guidance. He has been gone forty days and forty nights, which in biblical terms means a long time. He is nowhere in sight. Like a thundering herd, the people descend on Aaron, "Come, make gods for us, who shall go before us" (Exodus 32:1). Their survival brains are in a maximal state. Under emotional pressure, Aaron reacts in milliseconds. Hasty and thoughtless, he yields to their feverish anxiety. Gathering gold jewelry, he melts the precious metal and forms a golden calf to satisfy the people's need for tangible assurance. He pimps for the golden calf and makes a table for the offering of sacrifices. To sweeten the deal, he invites the excited crowd to return the next day for a foot-stomping feast. Appealing to their party-animal instincts, Aaron is prepared to proclaim, "Let's make Israel great again!"

Aaron is a pseudo-self personified, capitulating to the people's insecurity and fickleness. He does not stop and think and offer a contrast to their instinctual needs. He does not differentiate himself. His principles are suspended; his soul is marketed. Nobel Peace Prize winner Elie Wiesel contends that Aaron runs away from tension and confrontation. For him, it is "peace above all." Aaron chooses to be a leader who follows.

On the other hand, when his brother Moses returns and sees the abomination, he asks Aaron, "What did this people do to you that you have brought so great a sin upon them?" Pitifully spineless, Aaron takes no responsibility and blames the emotional tribe: "You know the people that they are bent on evil." Pseudo-selves who negotiate their actions are also willing to negotiate the truth. Wiesel concludes that Moses is a fervent believer in the truth, just as Aaron is a believer in expediency.

How many times do we see the same behavior in our corner of the world? We have witnessed a steady exposure of men who have bartered a potential benefit in exchange for sexual favors. The same quid pro quo has been part of congressional operation for centuries. Lest we be too poignant in our assessment, we function at this lower level ourselves, far more than we would like to admit. But the more the pattern continues, the more vulnerable we become to pseudo-selves who claim to have the means or rewards to take care of us. And we exchange our best thinking and functioning for their impressive promises. Duped, a segment of the population never gets its eyes back. They believe their rewards are in the making, the *quid* of the *pro quo* is coming. Disbelieving is hard work.

Uproar is not a prime time for mature adults to replace juvenile leaders. After all, the less mature are more impatient, enamored with their capacities to change things, and pawns of peer pressure. They, in a sense, thrive in Uproar. As psychologist Keith Payne reminded us, in uncertain and uneven periods, we are more vulnerable to the snake oil booster, the Houdini "wannabe," the fascist in Redeemer costume, and the alpha Messiah. I have combined these mythical images into the figure of the hero-warrior who offers thick promises and immediate results. In return for the magic, some will project greatness onto some celebrity, wealthy scion, or person of notoriety. Again, we have been reminded, this time by Daniel Kahneman, of the mental shortcut he called the "halo effect," the attribution of superhuman strength, wisdom, and unique ability to those individuals who have achieved lofty positions. Actually, we participate in a psychological Ponzi scheme. History has proven that these larger-than-life individuals have clay feet, bloated egos, and shaky identities. They slip on banana peels, place their bets on the wrong horse, and track manure on their feet into the house like the rest of us.

The question for each of us is, why do we become their "poodles" and lack backbone? Why are we negotiating away our integrity?

THREE WRIGHTS AND A RUSSELL

System theory contends that one's level of maturity, not flash and feathers, is what defines leadership. No system will rise above the level of maturity of its leaders. Leaders, therefore, work on their own development and growth. Leaders essentially seek to understand their own functioning, use principles to instruct action, and work on defining themselves.

When I offer presentations on leadership in emotional systems, I conclude with a section titled "Three Wrights and a Russell." I mention that they will not see the vocabulary associated with Bowen theory, but they can't miss the concepts, the way of thinking Bowen proposed. Ask yourself, is this how I think about leadership?

Wright One: In 1896, the Church of the Brethren in Christ met at an Indiana college for a convention. Bishop Melvin Wright convened the meeting with an invitation to anyone who might want to come forward and talk about the marvelous changes taking place in society. The president of the hosting institution accepted the invitation. He spoke glowingly of the many advancements, adding that he thought in the near future even flight would be possible for humans. Perturbed, Bishop Wright asked the president to be seated. According to the Bible, Wright insisted, flight was reserved for the angels. He would not condone heresy in his region. After the convention, Bishop Wright returned home, whereupon he was greeted by his two sons, Orville and Wilbur.

Wright Two: Near the end of his life, the noted architect Frank Lloyd Wright gave a talk to a group of selected young architects. Knowing the perpetual worry of emerging architects, whether to go with the latest popular style or to risk being imaginative, Wright spoke candidly about their becoming architects of their own lives:

> Consider that you, as young architects, are to be the pattern-givers of civilization . . . you must be the way-showers. As no stream can rise higher than its course, so you can rise no more or better to architecture than you are. So why not go to work on yourselves, to make yourselves in quality what you would have your buildings be?[3]

Wright Three: Frank Lloyd Wright designed a home for an industrial baron, built of the finest materials and with the greatest detail. One evening, however, a thunderstorm hovered over the mansion and a leak developed in the roof. The rainwater dripped onto the industrialist. Damp and irate, he called Wright, chastising him vigorously. Wright listened to his angry tirade and then asked, "Have you tried moving your chair?"

Russell One: At a dinner, Hall of Fame basketball player Bill Russell told this story of being in the eleventh grade:

I was cut from the junior varsity basketball team. Our varsity coach then approached me, and asked me to play on the varsity.

Stunned, I said, "I just got cut from the JV team."

His answer: "I'm not coaching JV."

The message for leaders: Being anxious (Bishop Wright), you lose perspective (you become dumber); you do not use the right lobe of your brain (blocking out new information). Leaders do their best thinking when they are not overly stressed (non-anxious presence) and can think about options (have you thought about moving your chair?). Leaders do their best work in being responsible when they work on themselves (be an architect in your life, a solid self). Being well defined ("I'm not coaching JV"), leaders express agency, display clarity, and stay connected. When our lizard brains are actively buzzing, emotional process is in full force. Uproar! The hero-warrior appears, the very one that Jim Collins warned us about. In Bowenian fashion, Collins would have us "Breathe. Calm Yourself. Think. Focus. Aim"—simply, *be* a *leader*.

THE LEADER'S NOTEBOOK

For a review (and a little fun), I have placed ten statements below. After each statement, put the number of the person on the list provided that you think most matches the statement. The pages in the book associated with each person are listed for you to turn to, if needed. An alternative would be to fill in the blank with a figure you think fits the statement. More than one person might fit each statement. Compare your responses with others.

The wit Will Rogers said that we learn through three methods: (1) reading, (2) observing, and (3) peeing on an electric fence. The first two methods are deductive, prevalent in this study. The third method is inductive, primarily experiential. This will be the real test of your learning—how you connect these ideas with the opportunities, challenges, and dilemmas of leading. But hopefully the first two instructional methods will aid your efforts to be a leader who does not "get dumb as fast," and you will become part of the special forces of leaders (the green berets) we need in this time of Uproar.

Statements

1. A self is more attractive than a non-self. ___
2. Taking responsibility for one's own emotional functioning, a leader is less apt to bargain away his/her principles. ___
3. To be a solid self, one has to have some courage. ___
4. A well-differentiated leader addresses emotional forces rather than the conditions on the surface, and consequently gets beyond the focus on symptoms to the underlying forces. ___
5. Mature leaders know that time is needed for things to process. Quick fixes appeal to the less mature who need their anxiety reduced. ___
6. The hero-warrior is caught up in appearances and pretension; the solid self practices agency. ___
7. When emotional forces rule our lives, we tend to connive, lie, and deceive in order to survive. ___
8. If one has to resort to justifying, explaining, or defending one's actions, the person usually turns to blaming others, accusing them as the cause of failure, verbally disparaging others, and shifting the view to others. ___

9. Mature people will give anxiety its due (provokes, prevents, upsets) but will not give it control of one's life. ___
10. When emotion mandates quick judgments, little time is available for looking at options or alternatives. But if the leader can retain autonomy and be independent of the turbulence, the leader can be more thoughtful, flexible, self-defined, and in touch with others. ___

List of Individuals

1. Frank Lloyd Wright, p. 147
2. Ernest Shackleton, p. 53
3. Green Beret, p. 20
4. Sister Georgina, p. 28
5. Heidi Martin, p. 74
6. Pierce Ralston, p. 91
7. Colby Wells, p. 105
8. Israeli soldiers, p. 49
9. Abraham Lincoln, p. 73
10. Constance Reed, p. 115

NOTES

CHAPTER 1: LIVING NOWHERE BETWEEN TWO SOMEWHERES

1. Charles Dickens, *A Tale of Two Cities* (New York: Heritage Press, 1938), 7.

2. Jean M. Twenge, *iGEN: Why Today's Super-Connected Kids Are Growing Up Less Rebellious, More Tolerant, Less Happy and Completely Unprepared for Adulthood—and What That Means for the Rest of Us* (New York: Norton, 2017).

3. E. O. Wilson, *The Social Conquest of the Earth* (New York: Norton, 2012), 7.

4. Jim Collins, *How the Mighty Fall: And Why Some Companies Never Give In* (New York: HarperCollins, 2009). Collins presents five stages of decline for organizations, labeling stage 4 as "Grasping for Salvation." It's a stage of near panic in which a desperate search is made for a charismatic leader or an outside savior. The sought-after "game changer" is part of the hero-warrior concept.

5. Joseph LeDoux, *Anxious: Using the Brain to Understand and Treat Fear and Anxiety* (New York: Penguin Random House, 2015). In a wide-ranging study, LeDoux distinguishes fear from anxiety, noting their different neurological pathways. As for treatment, he acknowledges being neither a therapist nor a physician. But being a neuroscientist, he has learned what happens in the brain when organisms are threatened.

6. George A. Akerlof and Robert G. Shiller, *Animal Spirits: How Human Psychology Drives the Economy and Why It Matters for Global Capitalism* (Princeton, NJ: Princeton University Press, 2009). The authors describe how people's economic

behavior is governed by less than rational choices. *Animal spirits* is a term referring to a restless and inconsistent way of functioning, certainly a lower-brain influence.

7. Daniel Kahneman, *Thinking Fast and Slow* (New York: Farrar, Strauss and Giroux, 2011). Kahneman reveals the results of his research on heuristic devices ("rules of thumb" or mental shortcuts) that the brain uses, predicating predictable biases in judgment. Not all faulty judgment can be attributed to the emotional brain's quickness. We use cognitive means to save efforts in thinking. Michael Lewis has written *The Undoing Project*, a history of Kahneman's and Tversky's relationship and scholarship.

CHAPTER 2: ANXIOUS TIMES

1. Rollo May, *The Meaning of Anxiety* (New York: Washington Square Press, 1950). In spite of its age, this volume still commands attention.

2. Alan Jacobs, *How to Think: A Survival Guide for a World at Odds* (New York: Currency, 2017). If I had more space, I would have devoted additional attention to the proposition Jacobs offers about how our thinking is impacted by the social groups to which we belong and the resultant "confirmation bias" in our thinking.

CHAPTER 3: SOCIETAL EMOTIONAL PROCESS

1. Barbara W. Tuchman, *A Distant Mirror: The Calamitous 14th Century* (New York: Knopf, 1978). Although the historian reaches into the distant past, she pinpoints what happens in societal emotional processes in terms of regression and the triggers of anxiety, such as disruption and uncertainty. Survival was pertinent, as a third or more of the European population died of the Black Death.

2. Murray Bowen, *Family Therapy in Clinical Practice* (Northvale, NJ: Jason Aronson, 1985), 371.

3. Scott Stossel, *My Age of Anxiety* (New York: Vintage, 2013).

CHAPTER 4: HEADS UP!

1. Elkhonon Goldberg, *The Wisdom Paradox: How Your Mind Can Grow Stronger as Your Brain Grows Older* (New York: Gotham, 2005). In addition to this volume, Goldberg's *The Executive Brain* and *The New Executive Brain* are extremely helpful in not only understanding brain functioning but also for learning theory.

CHAPTER 5: THE NON-ANXIOUS PRESENCE

1. John Gottman and Nan Silver, *The Seven Principles for Making Marriage Work: A Practical Guide from the Country's Foremost Relationship Expert* (New York: Brown, 1995). Gottman has not been appreciative of Dr. Bowen's work, but in my opinion Gottman has misunderstood aspects of Bowen theory. I think the two are closer than Gottman admits.

CHAPTER 6: IMPACTING THE EMOTIONAL SYSTEM

1. Edwin Friedman, *A Failure of Nerve: Leadership in the Age of the Quick Fix* (New York: Seabury, 1999), 68.
2. Seth Godin, *Tribes: We Need You to Lead Us* (New York: Portfolio, 2008). I find both Godin's books and blog to be stimulators of my thinking.

CHAPTER 10: ROCKING THE EMOTIONAL BOAT

1. Sherwin B. Nuland, *The Doctor's Plague* (New York: Norton, 2003).

CHAPTER 11: WE VERSUS THEY

1. Edward de Bono, *Conflicts: A Better Way to Resolve Them* (New York: Penguin, 1985), 25.

CHAPTER 12: STAYING CALM AND COURAGEOUS, NO MATTER WHAT

1. Having done extensive research on the influence of family functioning on one's self, Duke collected stories from hundreds of people and found that the stories coincided with the seven plots noted in Christopher Booker's book, *The Seven Plots: Why We Tell Stories*: (1) overcoming the monster—rising up to defeat a personal default or illness, overcoming a historical or natural disaster; (2) the quest—searching for the missing purpose or discovering the rule of life; (3) voyage and return—venturing into the unknown with the expectation that the return will be something that benefits the village or territory; (4) rags to riches—one can start low but end up high;

(5) tragedy—a suspenseful endeavor or a harsh condition ends in a tragic way; (6) comedy—a farce or ridiculous tale; and (7) rebirth—out of desperation, one prevails, one is "born again" or is transposed by events.

2. Duke's "Do You Know Scale" (DYK) can be found in his article "Knowledge of Family History as Clinically Useful Index of Psychological Well-Being and Prognosis: A Brief Report." *Psychotherapy: Therapy, Research, Practice, Training* 45, no. 2 (2008): 268–72.

POSTSCRIPT

1. Murray Bowen, *Family Therapy in Clinical Practice* (Northvale, NJ: Jason Aronson, 1985), 304.

2. Bowen, *Family Therapy*, 365.

3. Three of the stories given in "Three Wrights and a Russell" I have heard in public presentations. But the story of Frank Lloyd Wright and young architects appeared in a handout given to trainees in Dr. Friedman's workshop on emotional process. He presented it originally to the staff of Gov. Ann Richards in Austin, Texas.

BIBLIOGRAPHY

Alperovitz, Gar. *What Then Must We Do? Straight Talk about the Next American Revolution*. White River Junction, VT: Chelsea Queen, 2013.

Ashton, Kevin. *How to Fly a Horse: The Secret History of Creation, Invention and Discovery*. New York: Doubleday, 2015.

Bateson, Mary Catherine. *Composing a Life*. New York: Grove, 1989.

Booker, Christopher. *The Seven Plots: Why We Tell Stories*. London: Continuum, 2004.

Bowen, Murray. *Family Therapy in Clinical Practice*. Northvale, NJ: Jason Aronson, 1990.

Bridges, William. *The Way of Transition: Embracing Life's Most Difficult Moments*. Cambridge, MA: Perseus, 2001.

Brown, David O., and Michelle Burford. *Called to Rise: A Life in Faithful Service to the Community that Made Me*. New York: Ballantine, 2017.

Collins, Jim. *How the Mighty Fall: And Why Some Companies Never Given In*. New York: HarperCollins, 2009.

Comella, Patricia A., Joyce Biden, Judith S. Bell, Kathleen K. Wiseman, and Ruth Riley Sagan, eds. *The Emotional Side of Organizations: Applications of Bowen Theory*. Washington, DC: Georgetown Family Center, 1995.

Cozolino, Louis J. *The Neuroscience of Psychotherapy: Building and Rebuilding the Human Brain*. New York: Norton, 2002.

De Bono, Edward. *Conflicts: A Better Way to Resolve Them*. New York: Penguin, 1985.

Dickens, Charles. *A Tale of Two Cities*. New York: Barnes and Noble Classics, 2003.

Duke, Marshall. "Knowledge of Family History as Clinically Useful Index of Psychological Well-Being and Prognosis: A Brief Report." *Psychotherapy: Therapy, Research, Practice, Training* 45, no. 2 (2008): 268–72.

Dunkelman, Marc A. *The Vanishing Neighbor: The Transformation of American Community*. New York: Norton, 2014.

Friedman, Edwin H. *Generation to Generation: Family Process in Church and Synagogue*. New York: Guilford, 1985.

———. *A Failure of Nerve: Leadership in the Age of the Quick Fix*. New York: Seabury Books, 1990.

Gardner, Daniel. *The Science of Fear*. New York: Dutton, 2008.

Gilbert, Roberta M. *The Cornerstone Concept: In Leadership, in Life*. Falls Church and Basye, VA: Leading Systems Press, 2008.

Gladstone, Brooke. *The Trouble with Reality: A Rumination on Moral Panic in Our Time*. New York: Workman, 2017.

Godin, Seth. *Tribes: We Need You to Lead Us*. New York: Portfolio, 2008.

Goldberg, Elkhonon. *The Wisdom Paradox: How Your Mind Can Grow Stronger as Your Brain Grows Older*. New York: Gotham, 2005.

———. *The New Executive Brain: Frontal Lobes in a Complex World*. New York: Oxford University Press, 2009.

Haidt, Jonathan. *The Righteous Mind: Why Good People Are Divided by Politics and Religion*. New York: Vintage, 2012.

Heifetz, Ronald A. *Leadership on the Line: Staying Alive through the Dangers of Leadership*. Boston, MA: Harvard Business School Press, 2002.

Heifetz, Ronald A., Alexander Grashow, and Marty Linskey. *The Practice of Adaptive Leadership: Tools and Tactics for Changing Your Organization and the World*. Boston, MA: Harvard Business Press, 2009.

Jacobs, Alan. *How to Think*. New York: Currency, 2017.

Kahneman, Daniel. *Thinking Fast and Slow*. New York: Farrar, Straus and Giroux, 2011.

Kottler, John. *Leading Change*. Boston, MA: Harvard Business School, 1996.

Lasch, Christopher. *The Culture of Narcissism: American Life in an Age of Diminishing Expectations*. New York: Warner, 1979.

LeDoux, Joseph. *Anxious: Using the Brain to Understand and Treat Fear and Anxiety*. New York: Viking, 2015.

Lerner, Harriet. *The Dance of Fear: Rising above Anxiety, Fear, and Shame to Be Your Best and Bravest Self*. New York: Harper, 2005.

Lukianoce, Greg, and Jonathan Haidt. *The Coddling of the American Mind: How Good Intentions and Bad Ideas Are Setting Up a Generation for Failure.* New York: Penguin Random House, 2018.

Masterson, James. *Narcissistic and Borderline Personality Disorders: An Integrated Developmental Approach.* New York: Routledge, 1981.

May, Rollo. *The Meaning of Anxiety.* New York: Washington Square Press, 1950.

McGoldrick, Monica. *You Can Go Home Again: Reconnecting with Your Family.* New York: Norton, 1995.

Mischel, Walter. *The Marshmallow Test: Mastering Self-Control.* New York: Little, Brown, 2014.

Norman, Donald A. *Emotional Design: Why We Love (or Hate) Everyday Things.* New York: Perseus, 2004.

Nuland, Sherwin B. *The Doctor's Plague.* New York: Norton, 2003.

Palmer, Parker. *The Courage to Teach: Explaining the Inner Landscape of a Teacher's Life.* San Francisco: Jossey Bass, 1998.

Payne, Keith. *The Broken Ladder: How Inequality Affects the Way We Think, Live, and Die.* New York: Viking, 2017.

Peck, Scott. *People of the Lie: The Hope for Healing Human Evil.* New York: Touchstone, 1983.

Perkins, Dennis. *Leading at the Edge: Leadership Lessons from the Extraordinary Saga of Shackleton's Antarctic Expedition.* New York: Amacon, 2000.

Picoult, Jodi. *Sing You Home.* New York: Simon and Schuster, 2011.

Quinn, Robert E. *Deep Change: Discovering the Leader Within.* San Francisco: Wiley, 1996.

Ripley, Amanda. *The Unthinkable: Who Survives When Disaster Strikes and Why.* New York: Three Rivers, 2008.

Rogers, Everett. *Diffusion of Innovations.* New York: Free Press, 1995.

Slater, Philip. *The Pursuit of Loneliness.* Boston: Beacon Press, 1970.

Steinke, Peter L. *Congregational Leadership in Anxious Times: Being Calm and Courageous No Matter What.* Lanham, MD: Rowman and Littlefield, 2006.

———. *Teaching Fish to Walk: Church Systems and Adaptive Challenge.* Austin, TX: New Vision, 2016.

Stossel, Scott. *My Age of Anxiety.* New York: Vintage, 2013.

Surowiecki, Jim. *The Wisdom of Crowds.* New York: Anchor Books, 2004.

Taylor, Shelley E. *The Tending Instinct: How Nurturing Is Essential to Who We Are and How We Live.* New York: Time Books, 2002.

Tillich, Paul. "Unholy Dread." *Lapham's Quarterly* 10, no. 3 (Summer 2017).

Tuchman, Barbara W. *A Distant Mirror: The Calamitous 14th Century.* New York: Knopf, 1978.

Turkle, Sherry. *Alone Together: Why We Expect More from Technology and Less from Each Other.* New York: Basic Books, 2011.

Twenge, Jean M. *iGEN: Why Today's Super-Connected Kids Are Growing Up Less Rebellious, More Tolerant, Less Happy and Completely Unprepared for Adulthood, and What That Means for the Rest of Us.* New York: Simon and Schuster, 2017.

Wilson, Edward O. *The Social Conquest of Earth.* New York: Norton, 2012.

INDEX